Table of Contents

I.   Overview

This Guide, prepared by the Federal Trade Commission (FTC), is intended to assist attorneys counseling identity theft victims. It explains:

- common types of identity theft
- the impact of identity theft on clients
- the tools available for restoring victims to their pre-crime status.

Specifically, the Guide highlights the rights and remedies available to identity theft victims under federal laws, most notably:

- the Fair Credit Reporting Act (FCRA)
- the Fair Credit Billing Act (FCBA)
- the Fair Debt Collection Practices Act (FDCPA)
- the Electronic Funds Transfer Act (EFTA).

It also includes information and materials published by other organizations that address less common, more complex, and emerging forms of identity theft, such as medical or employment related identity theft.

II. Understanding Identity Theft and How to Assist its Victims

Each year, millions of Americans discover that a criminal has fraudulently used their personal information to obtain goods and services and that they have become victims of identity theft. Under federal law, identity theft occurs when someone uses or attempts to use the sensitive personal information of another person to commit fraud. A wide range of sensitive personal information can be used to commit identity theft, including a person's name, address, date of birth, Social Security number (SSN), driver's license number, credit card and bank account numbers, phone numbers, and even biometric data like fingerprints and iris scans.

New & Existing Financial Accounts

The most common form of identity theft, and the main focus of this Guide, involves the fraudulent use of a victim's personal information for financial gain. There are two main types of such financial frauds:

- **Using the victim's existing credit, bank, or other accounts**

  - A victim of existing account misuse often can resolve problems directly with the financial institution, which will consider the victim's prior relationship with the institution and the victim's typical spending and payment patterns.

- **Opening new accounts in the victim's name**

  - A victim of new account identity theft usually has no preexisting relationship with the creditor to help prove she is not responsible for the debts.

  - The new account usually is reported to one or more credit reporting agencies (CRA), where it then appears on the victim's credit report. Since the thief does not pay the bills, the account goes to collections and appears as a bad debt on the victim's credit report. Often, the victim does not discover the existence of the account until it is in collection.

  - The victim must prove to the creditor that she is not responsible for the account and clear the bad debt information from her credit report.

Many times victims experience both.

Other types of identity theft are listed in the Glossary.

The Goals for Victims

This Guide will help you assist a victim achieve three goals:

1. stopping or minimizing further fraud from occurring
2. proving that identity theft has occurred and that the victim is not responsible for debts incurred in her name and
3. correcting any errors on the victim's credit report to restore her financial reputation and credit score

The Guide initially assumes a worst-case scenario, where the victim has experienced new account identity theft, and a fraudulent new account has been added to her credit report. It presents simpler alternatives for victims who have not experienced new account identity theft and who typically do not need to clear their credit report.

Guiding vs. Hands-on

The Guide also assumes that many victims of identity theft are able to resolve their concerns on their own, once they have been told about the steps they need to take.

RECOMMENDED APPROACH:
Encourage most victims to take as many steps as possible on their own, and offer to stay in touch to monitor success and provide additional assistance as needed.

SPECIAL CASES:
In some instances, however, it may be clear from the initial screening call that the victim will be unable to undo the harms caused by the theft of her identity. Victims may need your immediate direct assistance when:

- their age, health, language proficiency, or economic situation create barriers for them in disputing and correcting errors in their records
- they are sued by creditors attempting to collect debts incurred by an impostor
- they are being harassed by creditors attempting to collect debts incurred by an impostor
- creditors or CRAs are being uncooperative
- their case is complex or involves non-financial identity theft

Vulnerability & Emotional Needs

Victims who have experienced the more serious forms of identity theft often report emotional harm, including feeling an enormous sense of vulnerability and a diminished trust in others. The Office of Victims of Crime has a tutorial on interviewing identity theft victims with tips on how to attune your approach to their emotional needs. You and those in your office who will be interacting with identity theft victims may want to go through the tutorial.

The Initial Screening Call

When a victim contacts your office, you will need to gather the facts to determine if identity theft has occurred, whether the victim needs your immediate direct assistance, and what assistance, if any, your office may provide. To make these determinations, ask the following questions:

- What facts lead the caller to believe that her personal information has been misused?
- How and where did the identity thief misuse the information?
- When and how did the caller discover the misuse or fraud?
- What harm has the caller suffered as a result of the identity theft?

First Steps with a Victim

If you confirm that the caller is an identity theft victim, advise her to take the following steps immediately to prevent further harm, whether the identity theft involves new or existing accounts:

1. place an initial fraud alert on her credit reports
2. obtain and reviewing her credit reports for evidence of additional identity theft and,
3. cancel any compromised bank, credit card, or other accounts

You also may wish to:

- provide the caller with additional resources, as described below.
- advise her of the importance of documenting her efforts

1. Placing an Initial Fraud Alert

Placing an initial fraud alert on credit reports will reduce the risk that an identity thief will open new accounts in the victim's name. An initial fraud alert stays on the victim's credit file for 90 days, and can be renewed every 90 days. Identity theft victims can place an initial 90-day fraud alert by contacting one of the following three CRAs. That CRA must, in turn, contact the other two CRAs on the victim's behalf:

Experian	Transunion	Equifax
1-888-EXPERIAN (397-3742) www.experian.com P.O. Box 9532 Allen, TX 75013	1-800-680-7289 www.transunion.com Fraud Victim Assistance Division P.O. Box 6790 Fullerton, CA 92834-6790	1-800-525-6285 www.equifax.com P.O. Box 740241 Atlanta, GA 30374-0241

> **Note:** A CRA may request additional proof of identity to place the initial fraud alert, and it may ask the victim to answer challenge questions—information in her credit report that only the victim would be expected to know.

If your client experienced new account identity theft, she should consider placing a credit freeze on her credit report.

2. Getting Copies of Credit Reports

Once your client has placed an initial fraud alert on her credit report, she is entitled to a free credit report from each of the three CRAs. These free copies of credit reports are in addition to free copy all consumers have a right to each year.

After placing a fraud alert on her credit report, your client should receive a confirmation letter from each CRA advising her how to order a free credit report. Some CRAs may allow the victim to place the fraud alert online. If so, she may be able to order and view her credit report online immediately upon placing the fraud alert. If the victim does not receive a CRA's confirmation letter, she should contact the CRA directly.

> **Note**: When a victim places a fraud alert on her credit report, the CRA may offer to sell her products or services, such as credit monitoring or identity theft insurance. For more information on these products, see "Identity Theft Protection Services".

> Later, when the victim calls the CRA to order the free credit report she is entitled to in conjunction with the fraud alert, the CRA may first direct the victim's attention to ordering her free annual credit report, before explaining how she can order the one associated with the fraud alert. This can confuse the victim and lead her to order the free annual report rather than the credit report that is hers by right after placing a fraud alert.

Victims should review their credit report for any accounts they did not open, debts they did not incur, and credit inquiries from companies they have not contacted. They should promptly contact any companies where their credit report indicates this has occurred and follow step 3 below. See "Disputing Errors on Credit Reports".

3. Contacting Creditors and Other Organizations

For each fraudulently opened or misused account, victims should:

- immediately contact the creditor's fraud department, not the customer services department

- explain the identity theft and direct the creditor to close the account and remove the charges

- ask if there is a specific mailing address to which the victim must send correspondence concerning the dispute of a debt, or to request documents related to the identity theft

FOR NEW ACCOUNTS

Where a new account was opened, the victim will need to prove that she did not create the debt. One method to prove new account identity theft is the FTC's Identity Theft Affidavit. However, some companies require victims to submit the company's own proprietary forms. The victim should ask each company she contacts whether it accepts the FTC Identity Theft Affidavit.

FOR EXISTING ACCOUNTS

Where only unauthorized charges to an existing account were involved, the victim should call the company for instructions. The detailed information in an FTC Identity Theft Affidavit or its equivalent should not be needed where only an existing account was misused.

Additional Resources

Based upon your conversation with the caller, you may discover that the victim has already taken the above three steps to address the theft. At this stage, determine whether the victim is willing to take additional self-help steps on her own with occasional phone support from your office, or seems likely to require hands-on assistance from your office in moving forward with the self-help process. Our checklist can help you figure out where your client is in the recovery process and what she needs to do next.

If the victim still needs to take the immediate steps, refer her to the FTC's step-by-step articles and checklists for the immediate steps to repair identity theft.

You may wish to point out additional educational materials and sample letters that she can use to address her situation.

There are other valuable online resources for attorneys and victim service providers as well.
Maintaining a Log

Whether the victim experienced new account fraud or existing account misuse, and whether she wishes to act alone or with your assistance, instruct her, from the outset, to keep a complete record of all:

- calls and letters she generates or receives
- the amount of time she spends and expenses she incurs in the course of her recovery

Documentation is critical for establishing the facts and providing a basis for damages should the matter go to litigation or criminal prosecution. Under federal law, victims may be able to recover the value of the time they spent recovering from the identity theft if the case is prosecuted in Federal court and the judge orders the defendant to pay restitution. A comprehensive sample record-keeping log is provided with the consent of the Victims Initiative for Counseling, Advocacy, and Restoration of the Southwest (VICARS).

Next Steps

In most cases, you may wish to schedule a follow-up call in about two weeks to see how your client's initial self-help efforts are going. Advise the client to contact your office any time if she has any questions or if her first self-help efforts are not fully successful.

Preparing for a First Meeting

2 week Follow Up Call

About two weeks after the screening call, you may wish to contact the victim to see how her efforts are paying off. Victims of existing account misuse who do not have exacerbating issues such as language deficiencies, pending lawsuits, or complex cases would rarely need to meet with you personally. For these victims, you can provide additional guidance during the follow-up phone call that will enable them to continue their successful self-help actions.

Victims of new account fraud – in addition to taking the three immediate steps discussed above – usually will have to take several more steps to address their problems. Specifically, they will need to write letters and create written documentation to continue resolving their problems. In some cases, victims will be able to do this on their own with only phone support from you.

If it appears that a victim may need help in executing some of the additional self-help steps, you may wish to arrange a first meeting, particularly if you want to assist the victim in preparing documents.

Before the First Meeting

To prepare for the meeting, advise the victim to gather supporting documents, including the following:

- government-issued IDs

- utility bills or other monthly statements showing the victim's address

- one or more credit reports showing fraudulent activity

- collection letters, credit card or bank statements, or any cards or merchandise received but not ordered

- a log showing any action that the victim may have taken to date

The Intake Meeting

The objective of the intake meeting is to determine the type and amount of assistance the victim may need and to develop an action plan. Our checklist can help you home in on what steps the victim has taken, what problems may have arisen, and what steps need to be taken next.

Get to Know Your Client

Understanding your client's identity theft experience is key to providing appropriate assistance. In addition to direct financial losses, some victims may have:

- suffered secondary harm, such as damage to their credit standing or to their reputation

- expended significant time attempting to correct credit reports and obtain new identity documents

- suffered revictimization, or chronic identity theft, whereby their stolen identity is used repeatedly by different thieves

- suffered severely debilitating emotional and physical effects, including depression, anxiety, and sometimes becoming suicidal

Review the Facts

The intake meeting provides an opportunity to review the facts gathered during the initial call. Specifically, determine what type of identity theft has occurred. Our chart provides sample interview questions that can help you get a better understanding of your client's situation. It also indicates the sections of the guide that relate to the type of identity theft your victim has experienced and the concerns she may be facing.

Make a list of additional documents that the client may need to provide, if the client did not bring all requested documents to the meeting or if it appears from the first meeting that additional documents are needed.

Making an Action Plan

Having determined the nature of your client's ongoing problems, explain to the tools and possible legal solutions available to address the identity theft. Your Action Plan should cover the following steps, as appropriate.

Documenting the Crime

If your client has experienced new account identity theft, the next phase in her recovery will be to document the crime. Such documentation will be necessary to prove to a creditor that she is not responsible for the fraudulent new account or to exercise certain legal rights, such as clearing fraudulent accounts from her credit report and prohibiting creditors from selling the fraudulent debts. Specifically, your client may need an Identity Theft Affidavit or an Identity Theft Report. Below are steps your client can take, alone or with your assistance, to prepare for obtaining these documents.

1. File a Complaint with the FTC

The first step in documenting identity theft is to file a complaint with the FTC. Your client can file a complaint online at https://www.ftccomplaintassistant.gov/.

Before filing her complaint, the victim should gather as much information as possible about the details of the crime. This would include a credit report from at least one of the three major CRAs, any collection letters or bills she received for accounts she did not open or charges she did not authorize, and any credit cards or other items she received, but had not ordered.

The complaint asks for the following information:

- the victim's full name, any other or previously used names
- current and/or recent address and the address at the time the crime occurred, if different from the current address
- Social Security number
- date of birth
- what the victim knows about who committed the crime or how her information was stolen
- what the victim knows about the fraudulent transactions, including institution names, types of account or transactions involved, account numbers, dates the accounts were opened or misused, and dollar amounts related to the fraudulent activity
- whether the victim has been able to obtain a police report, and if so, the details.

11

Note: It is important to note that victims are not required to file a written complaint with the FTC to pursue their legal rights to remedy identity theft. Victims who do not want to provide their personal information can file their complaints with the FTC anonymously.

Victims also have the option of filing a complaint by phone or mail, but will not receive a printed copy:

BY PHONE

FTC Identity Theft Hotline, toll-free: 1-877-ID-Theft (438-4338); TTY: 1-866-653-4261

BY MAIL

Identity Theft Clearinghouse
Federal Trade Commission
600 Pennsylvania Avenue, NW
Washington, DC 20580.

The FTC does not investigate or prosecute individual identity theft cases. The FTC enters the complaints into its Consumer Sentinel Network and makes them available to enforcement agencies throughout the country for their investigations. The complaints also help the FTC identify general trends in identity theft and violations of the FCRA.

2. Prepare an FTC Identity Theft Affidavit

Next, your client should prepare an Identity Theft Affidavit, which many creditors accept to dispute fraudulent new accounts. It also will assist your client in preparing an Identity Theft Report, as explained below.

By completing the FTC complaint online, your client will be then able to print a copy of her Affidavit, with most of the information filled in automatically. Specifically, after she has completed the online complaint's guided interview process and has hit the "Submit" button, a page will appear that will provide a link to print the Affidavit. Alternatively, victims can print a blank copy of the Identity Theft Affidavit. The Affidavit contains a block for notarization or a witness signature.

You may wish to fill in the Identity Theft Affidavit form by hand as you get to know your client and review the facts with her. Filling out a hard copy of the Affidavit as you interview your client serves dual purposes:

- You will gain a comprehensive understanding of your client's experience and identify knowledge gaps.
- You will provide her with a document to reference as she goes through the FTC's online complaint filing process, which collects much of the same information.

3. File a Police Report

The next step in documenting identity theft is to obtain an Identity Theft Report, which will enable the victim to:

- take advantage of certain rights provided under the FCRA
- obtain a company's business records related to its transactions with the identity thief

An Identity Theft Report is a police report that contains information specific enough for a CRA or creditor to determine the legitimacy of the identity theft claims. This usually is more detailed than a typical police report and best accomplished by filing a local police report and attaching or incorporating the information from the Identity Theft Affidavit.

Your client should bring a copy of her FTC ID Theft Affidavit, as well as documentation supporting her proof of identity and evidence of the crime. The goal is to get a copy of a police report that incorporates as much detail as possible about the facts of the crime. Your client can request that the police attach or incorporate her Identity Theft Affidavit to the department's basic police report form. There are signature blocks on the Affidavit for the victim and the officer.

If possible, your client should file her report with the local police in person. Police sometimes are reluctant to provide victims with a police report. Although some states require police to write reports for identity theft crimes, in other jurisdictions the officials may feel that they have higher priority matters to handle, or may not understand the importance of the police report in victim recovery. If your client has difficulty obtaining a police report, review the steps that she can take to obtain a police report.

Once your client obtains an Identity Theft Report, she will be able to prevent most further harm and restore her financial reputation.

Using the Documents to Effectuate Self-Help Recovery

1. Send Creditors and Other Organizations Written Dispute Letters

Victims should follow up their initial telephone calls to creditors with written dispute letters, including copies of their Identity Theft Affidavit.

On the initial phone call, your client should have asked if the creditor requires:

- the use of their own **dispute forms**

- the Identity Theft Affidavit to be **notarized**

- a **police report**. *A police report should not be required as part of this written dispute, but some creditors may ask for one.*

- a **specific mailing address** to which the victim must send correspondence concerning the dispute of a debt, or to request documents related to the identity theft. *If there are no designated addresses, your client should write to the company at the address given for billing inquiries, not the address for sending payments.*

Victims also may want to include in their dispute letters a request for business records, such as any applications and records of transactions between the identity thief and the creditor. The creditor can require a police report before it provides the requested transaction records.

She should send her letters by certified mail, return receipt requested, to document what the company received and when. Sample dispute and document request letters are available.

Once a victim resolves her identity theft dispute with a company, she should get a letter from the creditor or other institution stating that the disputed account is closed and the fraudulent debt discharged. This letter will be useful if errors relating to the account reappear on the victim's credit report, or if she is contacted again regarding the fraudulent debt.

2. Fix Credit Reports

Victims need to clear their credit reports of any accounts they did not open, debts they did not incur, and credit inquiries from companies they have not contacted. They should also correct any inaccuracies in their personal information—such as their Social Security number, address, name or initials, and employers.

There are two ways to address incorrect information on a credit report:

Victims can have inaccurate identity theft information permanently blocked from appearing on their credit report by using the streamlined procedures in section 605B and 623(a)(6)(B) of the FCRA. Examples of information victims might want to have permanently blocked include fraudulent new accounts they did not open, credit inquiries initiated by an identity thief, and additional addresses or other information that does not relate to them. Victims must obtain an Identity Theft Report that is verified by the police to use the procedures of section 605B and 623(a)(6)(B).

Victims can correct the erroneous information in their credit reports by using the dispute process available to all consumers under sections 611 and 623 of the FCRA. A correction might be preferred to a complete and permanent block when the account affected by identity theft is one that, when restored to its pre-crime status, would significantly benefit the victim's credit score. Another situation might be when the victim has closed the existing account that was damaged by the identity thief, and opened another account with the same company. In such a case, the favorable account history associated with the damaged account might be transferred to the new account.

3. Monitor Credit Reports

After fixing the errors in their credit reports, victims should monitor their reports for new fraudulent activity for the first year after the identity theft is discovered. Victims also can take advantage of the free annual credit report, and should consider staggering their requests among the three CRAs to receive one every four months so as to obtain more continuous coverage during the 12-month period. Victims with an extended fraud alert may use their second free credit report to continue their monitoring during the 12-month period after the alert was placed.

4. Consider an Extended Fraud Alert

Your client should consider placing an extended, seven-year fraud alert on her credit report. This will make it more difficult for an identity thief to open new accounts in the victim's name because potential creditors have to contact the victim by phone, in person, or by another means indicated by the victim before extending new credit, raising credit limits, or issuing additional cards.

The requirements for placing an extended, seven-year fraud alert differ slightly for each company. One requirement common to all companies is that the victim must provide an Identity Theft Report with her request for the extended fraud alert. Because not all police departments provide police reports to identity theft victims, the FTC's Rule on Related Identity Theft Definitions, 16 C.F.R. Part 603.3, specifies that a print-out of a Complaint filed with the FTC will suffice for obtaining an extended fraud alert. Company-specific information on how to obtain a seven-year fraud alert can be found at the links indicated below:

Experian	Transunion	Equifax
Mail: PO Box 9554 Allen, TX 75013 web info (including link to form)	Mail: PO Box 6790 Fullerton, CA 92834 web info (no form)	Mail: Information Services, LLC PO Box 105069 Atlanta, GA 30348-5069 web info (including link to form)

You may also want to consider placing fraud alerts with specialty CRAs, such as those dealing with offers of insurance or landlord/tenant issues.

Attorney Intervention

If your client can't take all of the recovery steps mentioned above independently, or continues to have problems after taking those steps, you may need to intervene on her behalf and directly contact the companies and entities involved. These entities may ask that you provide a Power of Attorney or other client authorization before discussing the victim's financial affairs. Our standard authorization form should satisfy these purposes.

Contact the Creditor or CRA

Depending on the nature and status of your client's issues, you may decide to communicate with your client's creditors or the relevant CRAs with a phone call, a letter inviting a phone call, or a letter requesting a written response. You can resolve some straightforward identity theft problems with a single phone call to the attorney or a senior supervisor at the company involved. Generally, it is preferable to communicate in writing to document your efforts. In some situations, however, immediate action is necessary, such as when a mortgage closing is being delayed due to the identity theft; in these cases, it may be preferable to contact the relevant parties by phone and follow up in writing, if warranted.

Sample Letters

Should you conclude that it is necessary to write to your client's creditors, this guide provides a number of sample attorney letters. You should know, however, that the sample attorney letters address only a small number of the potential problems that victims encounter. Further, the applicability of the different remedies available to identity theft victims under the statutes can be very fact-specific. Accordingly, adapt your letter to the particular circumstances of your client's complaint and be as specific as possible. At a minimum, insert a statement of the facts and an explanation of the remedies the victim is due. If the company's response has been inadequate, explain why the company is not meeting its legal obligations.

Closing Letter

Finally, you may want to provide your client with a closing letter summarizing the problems you worked on as her representative, the entities that you contacted, and the results you obtained. This will serve as a reference for both of you if your client is re-victimized and gets in touch with your office.

Private Rights of Action and Consumer Protection Remedies

This guide focuses on resolving victims' issues in a non-litigation context. The federal consumer credit protection statutes, however, provide private rights of action under some circumstances. Accordingly, review each applicable statute carefully to determine the scope and type of remedies that may be available to your client. These can provide remedies for violations, including compensatory damages, attorneys' fees, statutory damages, punitive damages, and/or injunctive and declaratory relief.

Many of the statutes provide for administrative enforcement at the federal and/or state level, either in lieu of or in addition to private enforcement. If you believe a creditor or CRA has violated the federal statutes discussed in this guide, please report this information to the Federal Trade Commission at www.ftc.gov/complaint.

Complaints filed with the FTC are available through the FTC's Consumer Sentinel Network to federal, state, and local law enforcement, including the banking agencies that regulate financial institutions.

III.　The Primary Tools for Victims

Explain to your client the key tools available to identity theft victims:

- fraud alerts
- credit freezes
- Identity Theft Affidavits
- Identity Theft Reports

This section can help you explain the tools and how they can remedy specific problems.

Primary Tools To Minimize Further Fraud

The primary tools for preventing the thief from opening additional new accounts in your client's name are the **fraud alert** and the **credit freeze**. In most cases of the more serious forms of identity theft, your client should place an initial fraud alert on her credit report as quickly as possible after discovering that she is or appears to be an identity theft victim, or she knows that her sensitive personal information has been stolen. Then she will have some time to consider whether to place an extended fraud alert or a credit freeze on her credit report. She also will be able to obtain a free credit report and review the report to see if it shows that there has been additional fraud by the thief.

Fraud Alerts

There are two types of fraud alerts consumers may place on their credit reports: an **initial** alert, and an **extended** alert.

INITIAL FRAUD ALERT

The Fair Credit Reporting Act (FCRA) gives the right to a consumer, or an individual acting on behalf of a consumer, to have a credit reporting agency (CRA) place an initial fraud alert on her credit report if she suspects she has been, or is about to be, a victim of identity theft. The consumer need only contact one of the three national CRAs, and that CRA will notify the other two, which will in turn place fraud alerts on the consumer's credit report. FCRA § 605A(a)(1), 15 U.S.C. § 1681c-1(a)(1).

- An initial fraud alert stays on a consumer's credit report for at least **90 days**.
- Consumers who place an initial fraud alert are entitled to **one free credit report** from each of the three nationwide CRAs. FCRA § 605A(a)(2), 15 U.S.C. § 1681c-1(a)(2).
- Potential creditors must use "**reasonable policies and procedures**" to verify the identity of an applicant before issuing credit in the consumer's name. FCRA § 605A(h)(1)(B), 15 U.S.C. § 1681c-1 (h)(1)(B). Note that even where potential creditors take reasonable steps to verify the consumer's identity, they may not always discover that the applicant is an imposter.

Extended alerts are available to victims of identity theft that provide the CRA with an Identity Theft Report. Because the risk of fraud is low, for this purpose the Identity Theft Report does not have to be filed in person with a law enforcement officer. A report generated by the police through an automated system, or a printed copy of the complaint the victim filed with the FTC (the Identity Theft Affidavit), is sufficient to obtain an extended fraud alert.

- An extended fraud alert stays on a consumer's credit report for **7 years**.

- Consumers who place an extended alert are entitled to **two free credit reports** within 12 months from each of the three nationwide CRAs. FCRA § 605A(b)(2), 15 U.S.C. § 1681c-1(b)(2).

- CRAs must **remove the consumer's name from marketing lists for pre-screened credit offers for five years**, unless the consumer requests otherwise.

- Potential creditors must **contact the consumer by phone** (or in another manner requested by the consumer) **or in person** before they issue credit in the consumer's name. FCRA § 605A(h)(2)(B), 15 U.S.C. § 1681c-1(h)(2)(B).

To place either of these alerts on credit reports, or to have them removed, consumers must provide appropriate proof of identity, which may include their Social Security number, name, address and other personal information requested by the CRA. Placing a fraud alert on a victim's file should not affect the consumer's credit score.

The presence of a fraud alert on a consumer's credit report may cause some delay if the consumer is trying to obtain credit. To limit possible delays, consumers may wish to include in their alert a cell phone number, where they can be reached easily. Consumers should be advised to keep all contact information in their alert current.

Credit Freezes

Many states have laws that let consumers "freeze" or restrict access to their credit report. When a consumer places a credit freeze, potential creditors and, in some cases, other third parties will not be able to get access to the consumer's credit report, unless the consumer temporarily or permanently lifts the freeze. This means that it is unlikely that an identity thief would be able to open a new account in the consumer's name. Placing a credit freeze should not affect a consumer's credit score.

Credit freeze laws and instructions vary from state to state. In some states, anyone can freeze his credit report, while in other states, only identity theft victims can. The three nationwide CRAs allow this right generally, even for residents of states that do not provide a specific freeze right. The cost of placing, temporarily lifting, and removing a credit freeze also varies. In many states, credit freezes are free for identity theft victims, while other consumers must pay a fee – typically $10. Unlike with fraud alerts, consumers cannot obtain a freeze on all three of their credit reports by placing it with one CRA. The consumer generally should place the freeze with each of the three CRAs, and pay the fee to each one.

Consumers who place a credit freeze will continue to have access to their free annual credit report and still will be able to buy their credit report and credit score.

Credit freezes only block companies' access with respect to **applications for new accounts**. The following parties still will have access to check your credit:

- companies with whom consumers already do business – for example, a mortgage, credit card, or cell phone company – and collection agencies that are working for one of those companies

- companies offering prescreened credit (unsolicited credit offers in the mail)

- potential employers, insurance companies, landlords, and other non-creditors

TEMPORARILY LIFTING A CREDIT FREEZE TO ALLOW A CREDIT REPORT CHECK

If consumers want to apply for a loan or credit card, or otherwise need to give someone access to their credit report, and that person is not covered by an exception to the credit freeze law, consumers will need to lift the credit freeze temporarily. They do so by using a PIN or password that each CRA sends when the consumer places the credit freeze. There may be a fee to lift the credit freeze depending on the state and whether or not the consumer is a victim of identity theft. The time it takes to lift the freeze also varies. Most states currently give the CRAs three days to lift the freeze temporarily. This might keep consumers from getting on-the-spot or "instant" credit, a fact that consumers may want to weigh.

Usually consumers do not need to lift the freeze for all three CRAs to get new credit. Rather, consumers should ask the potential creditor which CRA will be used and then lift the freeze only for that CRA.

What a Fraud Alert or Credit Freeze Does Not Do

Although both a fraud alert and a credit freeze can help keep an identity thief from opening most new accounts in a consumer's name, they do not resolve the threat of all types of identity theft. For example, it will not protect consumers from:

- an identity thief who uses a consumer's existing credit cards or other accounts

- new accounts, such as bank or health insurance accounts, that an identity thief might be able to open without a credit check

- other types of identity theft, such as medical or criminal record identity theft

- creditors who open a new account without doing a credit check

A fraud alert or credit freeze is effective only when the transaction involves pulling a credit report.

Primary Tools to Show That the Victim is Not Responsible for the Fraud and to Correct Credit Reports

Your client should be aware of the two primary tools for an identity theft victim to prove to creditors and other entities where the thief has committed fraud in her name that she is not responsible, and to correct her credit report: the **Identity Theft Affidavit** and the **Identity Theft Report**. Although their names and appearance are similar, these tools provide victims with significantly different rights.

The Identity Theft Affidavit

The Identity Theft Affidavit (Affidavit) is the primary tool for proving the victims' innocence to creditors and other entities where the thief has committed fraud in their names. It is a sworn statement that provides critical, detailed information in a comprehensive and standardized manner. It is widely accepted as a way for the victim to dispute fraud committed by the identity thief. Many of the sample dispute letters in this Guide recommend enclosing an Identity Theft Affidavit.

The victim should check with each company where she intends to use the Affidavit as part of her dispute documentation to determine if it accepts the FTC's Identity Theft Affidavit, or if it requires the use of its own proprietary Affidavit.

The victim either can print a blank copy from the FTC's website and fill it out by hand, or file an online complaint with the FTC and print it out filled in. Whether filling it out by hand or printing it from the FTC's online complaint system, the victim should first gather her information to provide as much detail as possible.

A completed Identity Theft Affidavit provides proof: 1) of the victim's identity; and 2) that she did not commit the frauds alleged in the Affidavit. However, it is understood that the victim may not know, and may have no way to ever determine, many of the facts and circumstances surrounding the crime. The victim should provide as much information as she can. A lack of knowledge about, for example, the perpetrator or how the information was stolen should not be held against the victim or invalidate the Affidavit.

Some companies require that the victim's Affidavit be notarized. Before signing the Affidavit, the victim should find out if the company requires notarization, and if so, wait to sign it in the presence of a notary. The victim should be aware that signing the Affidavit potentially exposes her to criminal penalties for filing false information, since the information may be shared with law enforcement.

For the purpose of disputing a fraudulent account that does not present any complicating factors, the company should not require a police report in addition to the Affidavit. If no police report is required, your client can leave blank the question regarding law enforcement. If the company does require a police report, your client should inquire as to the reason for the request. If the request seems justified, she should file a police report and fill in the Affidavit's section on law enforcement reports.

When filing the Affidavit with a particular company, the victim should consider redacting information related to accounts with any other companies. The victim should attach copies of her supporting documentation, as proof of her identity and to show that she is a victim of identity theft, and not the person who created the fraudulent accounts or transactions in her name. This would include copies of, for example:

- government-issued identification documents

- utility bills or other documentation showing the victim's current address

- a credit report marked-up to indicate which information is inaccurate as a result of identity theft

- any bills, collection letters, or other documents related to the fraudulent accounts or transactions

The Identity Theft Report

The Identity Theft Report is the primary tool for removing inaccurate identity theft-related information from the victim's credit report.

LEGAL DEFINITIONS OF AN IDENTITY THEFT REPORT

As defined in the FCRA, the Identity Theft Report is a report:

- that alleges an identity theft

- that is a copy of an official, valid report filed by a consumer with an appropriate Federal, State, or local law enforcement agency

- the filing of which subjects the person filing the report to criminal penalties relating to the filing of false information if, in fact, the information in the report is false.

FCRA Section 603(q)(4), 15 U.S.C. 1681a

Under the authority provided to it by Congress, the FTC modified the definition in several important ways. The FTC's Rule on Related Identity Theft Definitions requires the victim to provide as much specificity as possible, including:

- information about when the loss, theft, or misuse of her personal information occurred

- any information about the perpetrator

- the names of companies that furnished the information to the CRAs

- account numbers for compromised or fraudulently opened accounts

- any other information about the theft

The FTC's Rule also states that a CRA or furnisher may reasonably request additional information or documentation if the Report does not contain enough specificity for it to determine the validity of the alleged identity theft. 16 C.F.R. § 603.3(a)(3). Bear in mind that many identity theft victims do not know – and may never know – who stole or misused their personal information, how it was stolen, or other aspects of the crime. If the victim cannot provide these kinds of details, the police, CRAs, or furnishers should not consider the Identity Theft Report incomplete. For examples of reasonable requests for additional information, see the Commission's Rule on Related Identity Theft Definitions.

HOW TO CREATE AN IDENTITY THEFT REPORT

If the victim has obtained a detailed report from law enforcement, that document could serve as an Identity Theft Report. However, normally, a law enforcement report doesn't contain enough detail to be considered an Identity Theft Report. The FTC's Identity Theft Affidavit can be used to add detail to a police report. This puts the job of gathering and organizing the information about the crime on the party in the best position to obtain it the victim.

When filing a law enforcement report, the victim should:

- bring the completed Identity Theft Affidavit

- have law enforcement verify the affidavit

- have law enforcement incorporate or attach the affidavit to their report

An Identity Theft Report created in this method should contain sufficient detail to avert requests by CRAs or furnishers for additional information.

5 MAJOR BENEFITS TO IDENTITY THEFT VICTIMS:

- **Blocking fraudulent information from appearing on a credit report:** By submitting an Identity Theft Report to a CRA, a victim can stop the CRAs from reporting information resulting from the identity theft on the victim's credit report. The CRAs have up to four business days after they accept the Report to block the information. FCRA § 605B, 15 U.S.C. § 1681c-2.

- **Preventing a company from refurnishing fraudulent information to a CRA:** Once a CRA informs a furnisher that it has accepted a victim's Identity Theft Report that states the information the company furnished was caused by identity theft, the furnisher is prohibited from refurnishing that information to a CRA. FCRA § 623(a)(6)(A), 15 U.S.C. § 1681s-2 (a)(6)(A). The same prohibition on refurnishing fraudulent information to a CRA applies if the victim files her Identity Theft Report directly with the furnisher. FCRA § 623(a)(6)(B), 15 U.S.C. § 1681s-2 (a)(6)(B).

- **Preventing a company from selling or placing for collection bad debts that result from identity theft:** Once a CRA informs a furnisher that it has accepted a victim's Identity Theft Report that states the debts the furnisher reported in the victim's name resulted from identity theft, the furnisher is prohibited from selling those debts to another company for collection. FCRA § 615(f), 15 U.S.C. § 1681m(f).

- **Placing an Extended Fraud Alert:** Consumers need an Identity Theft Report to place an extended 7-year fraud alert on their credit reports. FCRA § 605A(b), 15 U.S.C. § 1681c-1 (b). For purposes of obtaining an extended fraud alert, an Identity Theft Report with a simple allegation that identity theft occurred should be sufficient.

Thus, victims can use police reports generated through automated systems, such as by telephone or computer, or the victim's Identity Theft Affidavit filed with the FTC. 16 C.F.R. § 603.3(c)(4).

- **Obtaining transaction documents from businesses:** Victims may obtain documents related to fraudulent transactions resulting from identity theft if they submit a police report, an FTC Identity Theft Affidavit (or other affidavit provided by the company), and proper proof of identification to the company where the fraudulent transaction occurred. FCRA § 609(e), 15 U.S.C. § 1681g(e). The statutory construction of section 609(e) is a bit unusual. While section 609(e)'s statutory language specifies a police report **and** an FTC or company-provided Identity Theft Affidavit, an Identity Theft Report that is comprised of an Identity Theft Affidavit attached to a police report, by definition, meets the section 609(e) requirements.

Police officers who participate in Consumer Sentinel, the FTC's nationwide online database of consumer complaints, can add the official police report number along with additional information about the Department to the complaint the victim filed with the FTC. The officer can retrieve the victim's complaint from the Sentinel database by searching for: the victim's Social Security number or their FTC Complaint Reference Number and one of four pieces of their personal information, such as name or phone number. The officer then can print the updated complaint. The police report and department-related information will be printed on the complaint the officer generates for the victim. There are signature blocks for the victim and the officer.

What to do if the victim cannot get a police report or a copy of the police report

Some jurisdictions may refuse to take police reports from identity theft victims. In other jurisdictions, a police officer may be prohibited from giving the victim a copy of the official police report. If so, the victim should consider the following options:

1. Provide the official with a copy of the Memorandum to Police on Importance of Taking Police Reports for Identity Theft. This document explains why an Identity Theft Report is critical for identity theft victims.

2. Check to see if the law in her state requires police to provide reports for identity theft victims. A map of the states that require the police to take reports from identity theft victims is at www.theiacp.org/idsafety/map.

3. Try to obtain a report from another jurisdiction, such as where the thief misused her information, or from a different law enforcement agency, such as the state police.

If the police take the victim's report, but are unable to provide a copy (refuse or unable by law or able to provide only a basic police report bearing a simple allegation of identity theft):

4. Ask the officer to complete the police report number and department-related information in Question 20, and sign her Identity Theft Affidavit. At a minimum, she should ask for the information to complete Question 20 on her Affidavit. The Affidavit, with the report number and as much information in Question 20 completed as possible,

and the basic police report, when available, attached, should satisfy the requirements of an Identity Theft Report

If the victim cannot file a report in person:

5. File an "automated report" on the Internet or telephone. Some jurisdictions only provide identity theft victims automated police reports bearing a simple allegation that an identity theft occurred. Victims who file automated reports often are provided only a written confirmation of filing and a report number, if anything at all. If the victim is using an automated police report to support a request for blocking information from her credit report, the CRA or furnisher could reasonably ask the victim for a completed, notarized Identity Theft Affidavit. To forestall that request, it is suggested that victims write the automated police report number on their Identity Theft Affidavit and attach the automated report confirmation notice (if any). 16 C.F.R.§ 603.3(c)(3).

If still unsuccessful:

6. File a Miscellaneous Incident Report in lieu of a police report. A Miscellaneous Incident Report is a document created by law enforcement to record non-criminal events or events that require no police action or follow up beyond the initial response. It is a report created for information purposes only. It does not generate a police report number, and it is not entered as a crime report into databases used for tracking a department's crime statistics.

If the victim cannot get any kind of police report from any law enforcement agency using the suggestions listed above:

7. Use the Identity Theft Affidavit filed with the FTC as an Identity Theft Report. In such a case, the victim should check the box under Question 23 indicating that she was unable to file any law enforcement report, and provide the FTC Complaint Number.

BACKGROUND INFORMATION

In the Analysis of Comments published with the Final Rule on Related Identity Theft Definitions (69 FR 63927, Nov. 3, 2004), the Commission observed that the fact that some police departments will not take identity theft complaints, combined with the fact that most federal agencies use automated systems to take reports, means that excluding automated reports generated by federal agencies would unduly burden victims of identity theft. The Final Rule contemplates automated reports generated by the FTC's complaint system as being within the scope of the definition of an Identity Theft Report.

When the victim does not want to file a police report

Sometimes a victim chooses not to obtain a police report, even though she cannot get the benefits of an Identity Theft Report without at least attempting to file a police report. Victims who do not want to file a police report cannot provide the CRAs with an Identity Theft Report. These victims should follow the dispute procedures under FCRA section 611.

IV. Addressing Account-Related Identity Theft

This section of the Guide deals with identity theft that involves the opening of new accounts or misuse of existing financial accounts.

Disputing and correcting fraudulent new accounts or the misuse of existing accounts and clearing fraudulent accounts from credit reports are among a victim's most critical steps in restoring financial health. This section of the guide sets out the two processes available to victims for disputing inaccurate information both with the credit reporting agency (CRA) and the creditor, debt collector, or other company that reported the information about its transactions with the imposter to the CRA (furnisher). Under the Fair Credit Reporting Act (FCRA), both the CRA and the furnisher are responsible for correcting fraudulent information in identity theft victims' credit reports.

Identity theft victims have the right to block the reporting of information that resulted from identity theft under section 605B of the FCRA. This provision requires the CRAs not only to block the information from appearing on the victim's credit report, but also to notify furnishers who reported the information it has blocked. This triggers section 623(a)(6)(A), which prohibits those furnishers from *continuing to report* that information to any CRA, and section section 615(f), which prohibits them from *selling, transferring or placing for collection* the fraudulent debts. Unauthorized inquiries on credit reports that were initiated by a creditor or prospective employer because of an application the imposter submitted also can be removed using section 605B. The section 605B blocking process requires the victim to file a police report.

If, however, the victim does not wish to file a police report, or if the victim wishes to correct erroneous identity theft-related information on her credit report rather than blocking the information entirely, she may use the FCRA's standard dispute procedures in sections 611 and 623 of the FCRA.

Identity theft may affect consumers in ways that are not covered by the FCRA. For example, the Electronic Fund Transfer Act and the Fair Credit Billing Act control certain activities of companies such as banks and credit card issuers. There may be instances where no specific federal law applies, such as disputes with companies that do not report account activity to the CRAs, including many telecommunication providers. In these circumstances, your client should, nonetheless, alert the company to the identity theft, and dispute the fraudulent charges or account activity.

Other statutes also come into play. The Fair Debt Collection Practices Act provides rights that could be valuable to victims of identity theft who face problems with debt collectors. And businesses that have entered into a transaction with an identity thief are obligated to provide without subpoena the identity theft-related documents to the victims and law enforcement officers investigating their cases under section 609(e) of the Fair Credit Reporting Act, also referred to as the business records turnover provision.

Blocking Information in Credit Reports (under Sections 605B and 623(a)(6))

Under section 605B of the Fair Credit Reporting Act (FCRA), both the credit reporting agencies (CRAs) and the furnishers (creditors, debt collectors, and other companies that reported the information) are responsible for blocking fraudulent information from appearing in victims' credit reports

Credit Reporting Agency Obligations

CRAs are required to block fraudulent trade lines (a line item on a credit report reflecting an account the consumer did not open or a transaction the consumer did not make) and other inaccurate information, such as unauthorized inquiries, that result from identity theft appearing on an identity theft victim's credit report. The victim must provide the CRAs with the following information in writing:

- a copy of an Identity Theft Report (filed with law enforcement)
- a letter explaining what information is fraudulent as a result of identity theft

    the letter should state that the information does not relate to any transaction that the consumer made or authorized

- proof of identity, which may include the consumer's Social Security number, name, address, and other personal information requested by the CRA

FCRA § 605B(a), 15 U.S.C. § 1681c-2(a).

CHECKLIST & SAMPLE LETTERS

- Checklist for the section 605B blocking request process
- Sample blocking request letter and attorney follow-up letters. Different information may appear in each of the three credit reports, so your client will need to customize her letters and attachments for each CRA.

IF THE CRA ACCEPTS THE IDENTITY THEFT REPORT

A CRA must block the fraudulent information the victim has identified within four business days after accepting her Identity Theft Report. When it accepts the Identity Theft Report, the CRA also must notify the furnishers of the fraudulent information that:

- the victim has filed the Report
- the Report states that the information they furnished resulted from identity theft
- it is blocking the information that they furnished

FCRA § 605B(b), 15 U.S.C. § 1681c-2(b).

The CRA may decline to accept the victim's Identity Theft Report if it reasonably concludes that the Report does not contain enough detail for the CRA to verify the alleged identity theft. 16 C.F.R. Part 603.3(a)(3). In that event, unless it is refusing to block the disputed information based on the criteria described below, the CRA is obligated to request additional information from the victim within certain timeframes, which are covered in the 605B Checklist.

16 C.F.R. Part 603.3(a)(3)(i) – (iii)

THE CRA MAY REFUSE

After reviewing the additional information provided by the victim, the CRA may refuse to block the disputed information, or it may remove an existing block, if it reasonably determines that the consumer:

1. has not told the truth about her identity theft

2. erroneously requested the block

3. acquired goods, services, or money as a result of the transactions identified in the blocking request

FCRA § 605B(c)(1), 15 U.S.C § 1681c-2(c)(1).

VERIFYING PROGRESS

The law does not specifically require the CRA to notify the victim if and when it accepts her Identity Theft Report and places the block, or that it has notified the furnishers of the situation. It must, however, notify the victim if it refuses to place or removes the block. FCRA § 605B(c)(2), 15 U.S.C. § 1681c-2(c)(2). To verify that the CRA has accepted the victim's Identity Theft Report and has placed a block, the victim should order a copy of her credit report two to three weeks after sending the blocking request to the CRA. The victim also should continue to monitor her credit report to see if the blocked information reappears, or for evidence that the furnisher has sold the debt to a third party for collection.

If you believe a CRA or furnisher has violated the provisions of section 605B, 623(a)(6), or 615(f), please report this information to the Federal Trade Commission at www.ftc.gov/complaint.

CRA Notification Triggers Information Furnisher Obligations

When a CRA accepts a victim's section 605B blocking request, it must promptly notify furnishers that their information has been identified as fraudulent in the Identity Theft Report. Such notification by a CRA triggers two obligations for the furnisher:

- the furnisher may not continue to report that information to any CRA
FCRA § 623(a)(6)(A), 15 U.S.C. § 1681s-2(a)(6)(A).

- it may not sell or transfer that debt to anyone else who would try to collect it
FCRA § 615(f), 15 U.S.C. § 1681m(f).

Note: Under the FCRA, a furnisher that is notified *by a CRA* that it has accepted the victim's Identity Theft Report **must** comply with the two requirements above. In other words, under section 605B(b) of the FCRA, the furnisher may not continue to report the blocked information, or place the debt for collection, when it has been notified by a CRA that the information is the result of identity theft.

Contacting the Information Furnisher Directly

In addition to filing an Identity Theft Report with the CRA, a victim also may file an Identity Theft Report directly with the furnisher that provided the inaccurate information.

A furnisher receiving a compliant Identity Theft Report directly from a victim is required to stop reporting the inaccurate information to the CRAs, unless it subsequently knows or is informed by the consumer that the information is correct. The furnisher is *not* required to stop any attempts to sell the debt to a third party for collection. FCRA § 623(a)(6)(B), 15 U.S.C. § 1681s-2(a)(6)(B).

THE FURNISHER MAY REQUEST MORE INFORMATION

A furnisher receiving an Identity Theft Report directly from a victim may decline to accept the Identity Theft Report only when it reasonably determines that it cannot verify the victim's allegations from the Identity Theft Report. It then must request additional information and documentation from the victim, within certain timeframes. 16 C.F.R. § 603.3(a)(3). The furnisher may specify an address for receiving Identity Theft Reports.

SAMPLE LETTERS

- Sample letter to furnishers regarding existing accounts
- Sample letter to furnishers from attorneys regarding existing accounts disputing inaccurate information on a credit report under FCRA section 623(a)(1)(B)
- FTC Notice to Furnishers

Sample letters from consumers and attorneys to furnishers request that the furnisher stop furnishing the disputed information under section 623(a)(6)(B), and enclose the FTC Notice to Furnishers referencing additional furnisher obligations that are triggered upon notification by a CRA that it has placed a block on the information provided by that furnisher.

VERIFYING PROGRESS

When the victim provides her Identity Theft Report directly to the furnisher, the statute does not require the furnisher to notify the victim if it ultimately refuses to accept the Identity Theft Report, or resumes reporting the disputed information. To remove this uncertainty, it is recommended that the victim's dispute letter **request an explanation of the furnisher's decision in writing**. The victim should monitor her credit reports after filing her Identity Theft Report with a furnisher to ensure that the disputed information does not reappear on her credit reports and that the debt has not been sold to another party for collection.

If the victim wants to avoid triggering the limitations associated with the provisions of FCRA section 623(a)(6)(B) and 16 C.F.R. § 603.3(a)(3) (*i.e.*, that the furnisher may a) sell the account for collection or b) request additional information from the victim unless or until the furnisher receives notification from a CRA that it has placed a block on the information provided by that furnisher), her dispute with the furnisher should not invoke the blocking process. She therefore should **not** include an Identity Theft Report in the written dispute she sends to the furnisher.

As long as the victim's Identity Theft Report and blocking request are accepted by a CRA, and the CRA notifies the furnisher, the victim will obtain the benefits of section 605B and 623(a)(6)(A).

> **Note on Private Rights of Action:** The FCRA provides a federal private right of action for violations of section 605B. Sections 616 and 617 of the FCRA set out the conditions under which federal law may provide for a civil cause of action, as well as the damages that may be available. Your client also may have remedies under state law.

Disputing Errors in Credit Reports
(Under Sections 611, 623(b), and 623(a)(1)(B))

Sections 611, 623(b) and 623(a)(1)(B) of the Fair Credit Reporting Act (FCRA) provide a dispute process that obligates both CRA and the furnisher (the company that provides information about the consumer to a CRA) to correct inaccurate or incomplete information in consumer credit reports. FCRA §§ 611, 623, 15 U.S.C. §§ 1681i, 1681s-2.

THE DIFFERENCE BETWEEN BLOCKING & DISPUTING

The blocking remedy in 605B, however, is limited to victims of identity theft. All consumers, regardless of the nature of their dispute, can use the 611 process outlined below to dispute incorrect information in their credit reports.

Contacting the CRA

The consumer should contact the CRA in writing to identify and explain the inaccurate information found in her credit report. CRAs must investigate the items in question – usually within 30 days – unless they consider the dispute frivolous. As part of this dispute process, the CRA also must forward all the relevant information the consumer provided about the inaccuracy to the company that furnished the disputed information. FCRA § 611(a), 15 U.S.C. § 1681i(a).

Furnisher Obligations

After the furnisher receives notice of a dispute from the CRA, it must investigate, review the relevant information, and report the results back to the CRA within 30 days. If the furnisher finds the disputed information is inaccurate, it must notify all three nationwide CRAs so they can correct the information in the consumer's credit file and promptly modify, delete, or permanently block the reporting of the inaccurate information. FCRA § 623(b), 15 U.S.C. § 1681s-2(b).

If the furnisher's investigation results in a change in the consumer's report, such as the deletion of disputed information, the CRA must give the consumer the written results of the changed information. Once an item is changed or deleted, the CRA cannot reinsert the disputed information back in the consumer's file unless the furnisher verifies that it is accurate and complete. If the CRA reinserts the disputed information, it must also notify the consumer that it has done so. FCRA § 611(a), 15 U.S.C. § 1681i(a).

Consumer Statements in Credit Reports

If, after investigating the matter, the furnisher believes that the disputed information is accurate, the CRA is not obligated to make a change to the consumer's credit report. Consumers can, nonetheless, ask the CRA to include a brief statement of the nature of the dispute in their file and in future reports. The CRAs may limit this statement to 100 words, or, they can use a code to indicate the nature of the consumer's statement. FCRA § 611(b)-(c), 15 U.S.C. § 1681i(b)-(c). Consumers also can ask the CRA to provide the statement to anyone who received a copy of the consumer's report in the recent past. FCRA § 611(d), 15 U.S.C. § 1681i(d).

Contacting the Information Furnisher Directly

In addition to disputing inaccurate information with the CRA, consumers may dispute inaccurate information in a credit report directly with the furnisher that gave the information to the CRA. Currently, filing a dispute directly with a furnisher does not afford consumers the same right as those associated with a dispute filed directly with a CRA, described above.

If a consumer notifies a furnisher directly in writing that information it provided to a CRA is inaccurate, the furnisher must review all relevant information provided by the consumer and conduct a reasonable investigation. This requirement does not apply in certain enumerated circumstances, such as if the consumer's claim is frivolous, if the consumer's dispute would be more appropriately directed to a CRA (e.g., if it involves information derived from public records), or if it comes from a credit repair organization. The furnisher must report the results of its investigation to the consumer. If the information is, in fact, inaccurate, the furnisher must report the correct information to the CRA. FCRA § 623(a)(1)(B), 15 U.S.C. § 1681s-2(a)(1)(B).

A dispute of inaccurate information made directly with a furnisher should be in writing and include supporting documentation. Many furnishers specify an address for filing disputes. If the furnisher reports the item to a CRA, it must include a notice of the consumer's dispute with the item. And if the furnisher determines that information is inaccurate, it may not report it again. FCRA § 623(a), 15 U.S.C. § 1681s-2(a).

SAMPLE LETTERS

- Sample consumer and attorney follow-up letters to CRAs and furnishers to dispute inaccurate information.

Note on Private Rights of Action: The FCRA provides federal private rights of action for violations of sections 611 and 623(b). Sections 616 and 617 of the FCRA set out the conditions under which federal law may provide for a civil cause of action, as well as the available damages. Your client also may have remedies under state law.

Disputing Fraudulent Transactions with Banks and Creditors

Your client's issues with companies and financial institutions may not involve removing or correcting information that appears on your client's credit reports at the three nationwide credit reporting agencies. The company may need to absolve your client's responsibilities for any fraud on existing accounts or any new accounts opened in her name.

Disputing Fraudulent Transactions with Check Verification Companies

Sometimes, identity thieves:

- open a checking account in a consumer's name, usually making an initial deposit with a counterfeit or altered check, and write checks that exceed the balance of the account

- steal a consumer's checkbook or preexisting bank account number and forge the consumer's signature or create counterfeit checks

Each of these scenarios can result in your client being linked to outstanding or unpaid checks at check verification companies.

> **Note:** In some cases, the thief's passing of bad checks may result in criminal charges being filed against your client. If your client appears to be a victim of check fraud-related identity theft, you may want to try to obtain a criminal background check on your client to see if any criminal charges were filed. If you can determine where the bad checks were passed, inquire whether law enforcement in that jurisdiction has issued a warrant.

WHAT ARE CHECK VERIFICATION COMPANIES

There are several credit reporting agencies (CRAs) that have check verification databases and collect information about consumers who have unpaid or outstanding "bounced" checks. Many stores and other businesses run an inquiry with such check verification companies when a consumer pays for merchandise or services with a check to see if the consumer is on the "bad check" list or has any unpaid or outstanding checks.

A check verification company is a "nationwide specialty consumer reporting agency" (specialty CRA) under the Fair Credit Reporting Act (FCRA) when it compiles and maintains information on consumers with outstanding or unpaid checks on a nationwide basis. Consumers may obtain an annual free copy of their consumer report from such companies. FCRA §§ 603(w) and 612(a)(1)(C), 15 U.S.C. §§ 1681a(w) and 1681j(a)(1)(C).

In addition, any store or business that refuses a check based on information from a check verification company must provide the consumer with an adverse action notice. FCRA § 615, 15 U.S.C. § 1681m. Should your client receive an adverse action notice, she is entitled to a free copy of her consumer report.

DISPUTING INFORMATION WITH A CHECK VERIFICATION COMPANY

If a victim discovers that an identity thief committed check-related fraud using her name, she should provide a check verification company with:

- appropriate proof of identity

- a copy of an Identity Theft Report

- identification of the fraudulent information

Then, the check verification company cannot report the fraudulent information to a national CRA. FCRA § 605B(e), 15 U.S.C. § 1681c-2(e). Unlike with credit reports at the three nationwide CRAs, consumers cannot use section 605B with check verification companies to "block" information related to identity theft from check writing history reports.

Consumers also may file a dispute if there is an error in the consumer report maintained by a check verification company. The check verification company, like other CRAs, is required to reinvestigate disputed information and remove or correct any information resulting from fraud or identity theft. FCRA § 611, 15 U.S.C. § 1681i. For more information about the CRA, see reinvestigation process under section 611 of the FRCA.

SAMPLE LETTERS

- sample consumer letter disputing information maintained by a check verification company

- attorney's follow-up letter for check verification company disputes

  Note on Private Rights of Action: The FCRA provides a federal private right of action for violations of sections 605B and 611. Sections 616 and 617 of the FCRA set out the conditions under which federal law may provide for a civil cause of action, as well as the damages that may be available. Your client may also have remedies under states law.

Disputing Fraudulent ATM and Debit Card Transactions

In some cases, identity thieves use an identity theft victim's lost or stolen ATM or debit card to make unauthorized purchases or withdrawals from the victim's account. Identity thieves also steal ATM or debit card account and PIN numbers by a practice known as "skimming," where the information is captured from the card's magnetic stripe, without the victim's knowledge, when it is swiped through a small electronic device called a "skimmer." The data is downloaded and used to create counterfeit cards or make online transactions.

A victim should notify her bank immediately if her ATM or debit card is lost or stolen, or as soon as she discovers that it has been used for unauthorized purchases or withdrawals. The extent of a victim's liability for unauthorized purchases or withdrawals on an ATM or debit card will depend on how quickly she notifies her bank of the loss, theft, or unauthorized use of the card.

LIMITS ON LIABILITY

The Electronic Fund Transfer Act (EFTA), and Regulation E, issued by the Board of Governors of the Federal Reserve, provide consumer protections for transactions involving ATM or debit cards and limit liability for unauthorized purchases or withdrawals using ATM or debit cards. 15 U.S.C. § 1693 et seq., 12 C.F.R. § 205. The EFTA sets forth three tiers of liability for unauthorized ATM or debit card uses:

- If the victim reports an ATM or debit card as lost or stolen **within two business days** after she realizes the card is missing, she will not be responsible for more than $50 total for unauthorized use. 12 C.F.R. § 205.6(b)(1).

- If the victim fails to report the lost or stolen card within two business days after realizing the card is missing or stolen, but does report its loss **within 60 days** after her statement is mailed to her, she could lose as much as $500 based on unauthorized transfers. 12 C.F.R. § 205.6(b)(2).

- If the victim fails to report an unauthorized transfer within 60 days after her statement is mailed, she risks unlimited loss and could lose all the money in her account and the unused portion of her maximum line of credit established for overdrafts. 12 C.F.R. § 205.6(b)(3).

If extenuating circumstances, such as lengthy travel or illness, prevent the victim from notifying the financial institution within the time periods described, the card-issuing financial institution must reasonably extend the notification period. 12 C.F.R. § 205.6(b)(4).

> **Note:** Many companies have adopted policies where they generally will not hold the victim responsible for the minimal liability amounts.

State laws, business practices, and contract provisions may impose lower liability limits than those contained in the EFTA. Review the laws and contract provisions to determine the full extent of your client's liability. In addition, the UCC, which does not generally apply to electronic transfers, may provide for consequential damages should the bank cause an unauthorized electronic withdrawal from a victim's account that results in insufficient funds. U.C.C. § 4-402.

CORRECTING ERRORS WITH ATM & DEBIT CARDS

In the event of an error in the victim's account because of a fraudulent transaction or the unauthorized use of an ATM or debit card, she should

- ❏ promptly call the financial institution and point out the error, no later than 60 days after the statement containing the error was sent

- ❏ follow-up in writing, by certified letter, return receipt requested, to prove the institution received notice of the error

After receiving notification of the problem, the financial institution has 10 days to investigate, must inform the victim of the results within three business days after completing the investigation, and must correct inaccurate information. 12 C.F.R. § 205.11(c).

The 10-day investigatory period may be extended to 45 days if the institution is unable to complete the investigation within 10 days; however, the institution must provisionally credit the victim's account in the amount of the alleged error within 10 days of receipt of notice of the error from the victim. 12 C.F.R. § 205.11(c)(2). In addition, a financial institution may extend the period from ten to 20 days if the notice of error concerns certain new accounts, or from 45 to 90 days if the notice of error concerns a foreign electronic fund transfer or a point-of-sale debit card transaction. 12 C.F.R. § 205.11(c)(3). An institution must correct any errors within one business day after determining that an error occurred. 12 C.F.R. § 205.11(c).

Victims are only required to take "steps reasonably necessary to provide the institution with the pertinent information" regarding the unauthorized use of ATM or debit cards. 12 C.F.R. § 205.6(b)(5)(i).

SAMPLE LETTERS

- sample victim's letter notifying a financial institution of a lost or stolen card, or one that was used for an unauthorized transaction, that consumers should contact their bank by phone as soon as they become aware of a missing ATM card.

- sample attorney follow-up letter, requesting the restoration of funds after an unauthorized transaction and an investigation period of 10 days,

- sample attorney follow-up letter requesting the restoration of funds after an unauthorized transaction and an investigation period of 45 days.

Note on Private Rights of Action: Section 915 of the EFTA provides a federal private right of action for violations of the provisions discussed above. EFTA § 915, 15 U.S.C. § 1693m.

Credit Card Issuer Obligations under the Fair Credit Billing Act

Identity thieves often make unauthorized charges on consumers' credit card accounts. This may happen either when they steal the actual credit card or obtain the credit card number through other means. Victims of identity theft then would have errors on their credit card statements caused by these unauthorized charges.

The Fair Credit Billing Act, 15 U.S.C. § 1601, (FCBA) establishes procedures for resolving billing errors on consumer credit card accounts, including fraudulent charges on accounts that have been caused by identity theft. FCBA §§ 161-162, 15 U.S.C. §§ 1666-1666a.

Note: The FCBA applies only to "open ended" credit accounts, such as credit cards and revolving charge accounts (e.g. department store accounts). It does not cover installment contracts, such as loans or extensions of credit that consumers repay on a fixed schedule.

LIMITS ON LIABILITY

The FCBA limits liability for unauthorized credit card charges to a maximum of $50 per card.

CORRECTING ERRORS WITH CREDIT CARDS

To trigger the FCBA's protections, a victim must send a notice of the billing error to the creditor or card issuer ("creditor") within **60 days after the first bill containing the error was mailed**. 12 C.F.R. § 226.13(b)(1). Victims should:

- write to the creditor at the address given for "billing inquiries," not the address for sending payments

- include name, address, account number, and a description of the billing error, including the amount and date of the error
- include copies of their police report, Identity Theft Affidavit, or other documents that support their position, and keep copies of their dispute letters
- send their letters by certified mail, and request return receipts, to prove the date the creditors received the letters

If an identity thief changed the address on the victim's account and the victim did not receive the bill, the victim's dispute letter still must reach the creditor within 60 days of when the creditor would have mailed the bill. This is one reason it is essential for victims to keep track of their billing statements, and follow up quickly if their bills do not arrive on time.

The creditor must acknowledge the victim's complaint in writing within 30 days after receiving it, unless the problem has been resolved. The creditor must resolve the dispute within two billing cycles (but not more than 90 days) after receiving the victim's letter. 12 C.F.R. § 226.13(c)(1).

During the dispute:

- victims may withhold the disputed amount (and related charges)
- victims must pay any part of the bill not in question, including finance charges on the undisputed amount
- the creditor may not take legal or other action to collect on the disputed amount and related charges during the investigation. 12 C.F.R. § 226.13(d)(1)
- the creditor may not threaten to damage the victim's credit rating or report the victim as delinquent while the bill is in dispute. 12 C.F.R. § 226.13(d)(2)

SAMPLE LETTERS

- Consumer letter to credit card companies
- Attorney follow-up letter to credit card companies

POSSIBLE OUTCOMES

If the victim's bill contains an error, the creditor must explain to the victim in writing how it will correct the victim's account. In addition to crediting the account, the creditor must remove and forgive all finance charges, late fees or other charges related to the error. 12 C.F.R. § 226.13(e)(1).

If the creditor determines that the victim owes a portion of the disputed amount, it must provide the victim with a written explanation. 12 C.F.R. § 226.13(g)(1) and Official Staff Commentary on § 226.13(g). The victim may request that the creditor provide copies of documents that purportedly prove that she owes the money.

Similarly, if the creditor determines that the entire bill is correct, it must tell the victim promptly and in writing how much she owes and why. 12 C.F.R. § 226.13(f). The victim may ask for copies of relevant documents. At this point, she will owe the disputed amount, plus any finance charges that accumulated while the amount was in dispute. The victim also may have to pay the minimum amount she missed paying because of the dispute. 12 C.F.R. § 226.13(g). The victim must be told in writing when payment is due.

If an identity theft victim disagrees with the results of the investigation, she may write to the creditor, but she must act within 10 days after receiving the explanation. The victim also may indicate that she refuses to pay the disputed amount. 12 C.F.R. § 226.13(g). At this point, the creditor may begin collection procedures. However, if the creditor reports the victim to a credit reporting agency as delinquent, the report also must state that the identity theft victim does not think she owes the money. The creditor also must tell the victim who receives these reports. 12 C.F.R. § 226.13(g)(4)(ii).

Any creditor who fails to follow the settlement procedure may not collect the amount in dispute, or any related finance charges, up to $50, even if the bill turns out to be correct and the bill plus finance charges are more than $50. 15 U.S.C. § 1666(e). For example, if a creditor acknowledges a victim's complaint in 45 days, 15 days too late - or takes more than two billing cycles to resolve a dispute − the $50 penalty applies. The $50 penalty also applies if a creditor threatens to report – or improperly reports – the victim's failure to pay to anyone during the dispute period.

> **Note on Private Rights of Action:** Section 130 of the Truth in Lending Act provides a federal private right of action for violations of the provisions of the FCBA described above. TILA § 130, 15 U.S.C. § 1640.

Disputing Unauthorized Charges and New Accounts with Other Creditors

Although credit card and bank accounts are favorites for identity thieves, they also target other types of credit accounts, such as those for telephone, wireless, cable, internet, gasoline, apartment leases, and utility service. Identity thieves may:

- open new accounts in the victim's name for such services or

- place unauthorized charges on the victim's existing accounts

These other types of accounts may not trigger the same set of rights for consumers. For example, some utility and other service providers may not provide information to credit reporting agencies (CRAs). In such cases, these companies are not furnishers and therefore are not covered by the Fair Credit Reporting Act (FCRA). Nor are they subject to banking laws or regulations. Nonetheless, identity theft victims are not without remedies.

Even without specific statutory remedies, identity theft victims can still dispute fraudulent accounts using general dispute procedures. The Identity Theft Affidavit is a generic form, available from the FTC's website, which many businesses accept from victims who are trying to establish account fraud.

> **Note:** Although many companies accept the Identity Theft Affidavit to prove account fraud, others require that the victim submit additional or different documents. Before

your client submits an Identity Theft Affidavit, she should contact each company involved to determine whether the company will accept it.

When submitting a dispute letter and Identity Theft Affidavit to a company, your client should:

- attach copies of any supporting documents, such as proof of identity and any billing statements or collection letters she has received

- send the materials to the address designated by the company for receiving such disputes. If there is no designated address, she should write to the company at the address for "billing inquiries," not the address for sending payments

- send the letters by certified mail with a return receipt requested, to document receipt and delivery date of the documents

SAMPLE LETTERS

- Consumer dispute letters for existing accounts

- Consumer dispute letter for new accounts

  Both letters request an investigation and correction, that the account be closed, that the victim not be held liable for the disputed debt, and that the company not sell the debt to another party for collection.

- Attorney follow-up letter

Dealing with Debt Collectors Seeking Payment for Accounts Opened or Misused by an Identity Thief

Consumers often learn they are the victim of identity theft when they are contacted by debt collectors about bills the consumers know nothing about. The Fair Debt Collection Practices Act (FDCPA) provides rights that could be valuable to victims of identity theft who face problems with debt collectors. 15 U.S.C. § 1692 *et seq.* Some additional rights are provided by the Fair Credit Reporting Act (FCRA). 15 U.S.C. § 1681 *et seq.*

Within five days after a debt collector first contacts the consumer, such as through a phone call, the collector must send the consumer:

- a written notice stating the amount of money owed

- the name of the creditor to whom money is owed

- what action to take if the consumer believes money is not owed. FDCPA § 809(a), 15 U.S.C. § 1692g(a)

If the consumer sends a letter disputing all or part of the debt within 30 days after she receives the written notice, the collector must stop trying to collect the debt. However, the collector is permitted to renew collection activities if it sends the victim verification of the debt, such as a copy of a bill for the amount owed. FDCPA § 809(b), 15 U.S.C. § 1692g(b).

STOP CONTACT FROM DEBT COLLECTORS

Identity theft victims can permanently stop a debt collector from further contacts by sending a letter telling them to stop. FDCPA § 805(c), 15 U.S.C. § 1692c(c). Other than to comply with section 615(g)(2) of the FCRA, described below, once the collector receives the victim's letter, it may not contact the victim again except to say there will be no further contact or to notify the victim that the debt collector or the creditor intends to take some specific action. FDCPA § 805(c), 15 U.S.C. § 1692c(c).

Note, however, that sending such a letter to a collector **does not eliminate the debt** and will not prevent the debt collector or creditor from taking other actions to collect the debt, including suing to collect the debt, unless the victim has also invoked his rights under the FCRA, as described below. Such a letter also does not prevent subsequent debt collectors whom the creditor may hire from contacting the victim.

PREVENT THE SALE OR TRANSFER OF THE DEBT

To prevent the debt collector from selling or transferring the debt or placing it for collection, the victim must notify the credit reporting agencies (CRAs) about the fraudulent debt, using the credit report blocking provisions of section 605B of the FCRA.

Upon accepting the victim's Identity Theft Report, a CRA must promptly notify the debt collector that furnished the information that the disputed debt may be the result of identity theft and that an Identity Theft Report has been filed. FCRA § 605B(b), 15 U.S.C. § 1681c-2(b). Debt collectors who have received such a notification from a CRA may not sell or transfer the debt or place it for collection, FCRA § 615(f)(1), 15 U.S.C. § 1681m(f)(1), and may not continue to report that information to a CRA, FCRA § 623(a)(6)(A), 15 U.S.C. § 1681s-2(a)(6)(A).

ADDITIONAL DEBT COLLECTOR OBLIGATIONS

Further, under section 615(g)(2) of the FCRA, when the victim or a CRA notifies the debt collector of the identity theft, the debt collector must notify the initial creditor that the debt may be fraudulent. If the victim requests, it must provide information about the underlying suspect transaction, as she otherwise would be entitled under FDCPA § 809(b), 15 U.S.C. §1692g(b). Examples of the kinds of information debt collectors might provide include:

- the name of the original creditor if different from the current owner of the debt

- a copy of the signed credit application

- the amount of the debt when it became delinquent

SAMPLE LETTERS

- consumer letter to debt collector

- attorney follow-up letter to debt collector

    Note: To prevent further resale of the debt, your client may wish to file a blocking request and Identity Theft Report under section 605B with each of the CRAs stating that the debt is the result of identity theft.

Note on Private Rights of Action: The FDCPA provides a federal private right of action for violation of any of its provisions. Section 813 of the FDCPA sets out the conditions under which a federal civil cause of action may arise, and the damages and penalties that may be available. FDCPA § 813, 15 U.S.C. 1692(k). Be aware that your client may also have private remedies under state law.

Obtaining Business Records Relating to Identity Theft

Identity theft victims are entitled to copies of transaction records relating to the theft of their identity, such as applications for credit, under section 609(e) of the Fair Credit Reporting Act (FCRA). 15 U.S.C. § 1681g(e). These documents can be essential in establishing the underlying fraud. Victims also can authorize law enforcement officers to receive the records directly from businesses without the need to obtain a subpoena.

Businesses that have provided credit, goods, or services to, accepted payment from, or otherwise entered into a transaction with someone who is believed to have fraudulently used another person's identification are obligated to provide such documents (free of charge, within 30 days) under section 609(e). Depending on the company involved, this provision is enforced by the Federal Trade Commission, Office of Thrift Supervision, Office of the Comptroller of the Currency, Federal Deposit Insurance Corporation, Federal Reserve, or National Credit Union Administration.

The types of documents the business must provide include "applications and transaction records" that were maintained by the business, or by another entity acting on its behalf, that relate to any transaction alleged to be a result of identity theft. The records could include invoices, credit applications, or account statements, and may include electronic records. There are no recordkeeping procedures in the statute, so if the business disposes of certain records regularly, they may not be available to the victim or law enforcement.

All requests under the provision by the victim or an authorized law enforcement officer on behalf of the victim must be in writing. The business may specify an address to receive these requests. Before submitting such a request, the victim should contact the business to verify the address to which she should send the request.

SAMPLE LETTERS

- consumer request letter
- law enforcement request letter
- attorney follow-up letter

THE BUSINESS MAY REQUEST MORE INFORMATION

The business may ask the victim to provide:

- the transaction date or account number if she knows it

- proof of the victim's identity, like a copy of a government-issued ID card

- proof of the identity theft, like a police report and completed Identity Theft Affidavit

   In most cases, the victim can use her Identity Theft Report, given that it contains both a police report and an Identity Theft Affidavit, to satisfy the proof of identity theft requirement. In some cases, the business may specify that the victim use the company's own affidavit for this purpose.

Businesses are protected from civil liability under any federal, state, or other laws for providing the records as long as the disclosure was made in good faith under section 609(e). FCRA § 609(e)(7), 15 U.S.C. § 1681g(e)(7).

Businesses may refuse to provide records if:

- they cannot verify the true identity of the person making the request

- the request for information is based on a misrepresentation

- the information requested is "Internet navigational data" or similar information about an identity thief's visit to a website or online service

    FCRA § 609(e)(5), 15 U.S.C. § 1681g(e)(5).

- state or other federal laws prohibit them from doing so.

    FCRA § 609(e)(9), 15 U.S.C. § 1681g(e)(9).

However, a business may not deny the records based on the financial privacy provisions of the Gramm-Leach-Bliley Act. 15 U.S.C. § 6803.

In the event that the business refuses to provide the records, it is recommended that the business communicate the reasons for the refusal to the victim or law enforcement officer or agency that made the request.

If your client has satisfied all of the section 609(e) requirements, and having received your follow-up letter, the business continues to refuse, the FTC would appreciate being notified of this fact. We ask that you, the attorney, please notify the FTC by email at "."

> **Note on Private Rights of Action:** The FCRA does not provide a federal private right of action for violations of section 609(e). Your client may have civil remedies under state law.

V. Addressing Other Forms of Identity Theft

Identity theft comes in many forms, many of which do not fall within the Federal Trade Commission's jurisdiction or are not covered by the federal statutes addressed in the previous Sections of this Guide. There are, however, resources to help identity theft victims resolve these less common forms of identity theft.

> **Note:** The FTC acknowledges the Identity Theft Resource Center, the Privacy Rights Clearinghouse, the Department of Education, and the Internal Revenue Service for their contributions to this section of the Guide. Contact those organizations directly with questions and for updates to their materials.

Identity Theft & Children

Child identity theft occurs when a thief uses a child's identity information to commit fraud. Most parents and guardians don't expect their youngster to have a credit file, and as a result, rarely request a child's credit report, let alone review it for accuracy. A thief who steals a child's information may use it for many years before the crime is discovered. The victim may learn about the theft years later, when applying for a loan, apartment, or job.

The FTC provides step-by-step guidance to address child identity theft.

Criminal Identity Theft

Criminal identity theft occurs when an imposter gives another person's name and personal information, such as a drivers' license, date of birth, or Social Security number (SSN) to a law enforcement officer during an investigation or upon arrest. Some victims, unaware of the earlier criminal activity by the imposter, may learn of the impersonation when the victim is unexpectedly detained, arrested, denied employment, or terminated from employment.

The Privacy Rights Clearinghouse provides guidance to address criminal identity theft. The FTC also provides step-by-step guidance on clearing your name of criminal charges resulting from identity theft.

Identity Theft Involving Federal Student Loans

In some cases, identity thieves get student loans in other people's names. The following information discusses the particular issues that arise with respect to federal student loans from Federal Family Education Loan (FFEL) and William D. Ford Federal Direct Loan (Direct Loan) program loans disbursed after Jan. 1, 1986.

How to Dispute the Fraudulent Loan

Regulations governing FFEL and Direct Loan programs provide that a loan may be discharged if it was falsely certified, e.g., obtained, as a result of identity theft. (See 34 CFR 682.402(e)(14) and 685.215(c)(4) . The regulations specify how a victim must prove the identity theft to the holder of the loan. Currently, there is no separate form for the identity theft discharge request.

Disputing a fraudulent student loan is more demanding than for other types of fraud. For example, a copy of a police report is not enough to support discharge of a loan on the basis of identity theft. Rather, clients must certify that they did not sign the promissory note or receive benefit of the loan; they might also be asked to provide a copy of a court verdict or judgment that determined they were a victim of identity theft.

If your client is unable to provide a court document that expressly states that the loan was made as a result of identity theft, she must provide other evidence of the fraud. In most cases, authentic signature specimens and other means of identification corresponding to the means of identification falsely used to obtain the loan will suffice. Regulations at 34 CFR 682.402(e)(14)(ii)(A) and (B) give examples of identifying information, including name, Social Security number, date of birth, official State or government issued driver's license or identification number, alien registration number, passport number or taxpayer identification number, as well as unique biometric data.

If your client cannot provide proof of the crime of identity theft, she may qualify for discharge under other provisions of 34 CFR 682.402 or 685.215 (e.g., false certification of eligibility to borrow or unauthorized disbursement). In those cases, 34 CFR 682.402(3) and 685.215(c) specify information needed to prove eligibility for the discharge. For example, the loan holder will ask the victim to present detailed documents proving the loan is eligible for a discharge. The documents might include a sworn statement and several samples of the victim's handwriting.

RESOLUTION

When the loan holder is satisfied that the loan was certified as a result of identity theft, the holder then will make corrections to:

- its own records
- the victim's credit record
- the National Student Loan Data System (NSLDS)

You can find loan holder contact information on billing statements and related lender correspondence. If the victim is unsure who holds the loan, she may call the Federal Student Aid Information Center at 1-800-4-FED-AID or check NSLDS at www.nslds.ed.gov to find out.

Assistance from the Department of Education

If the loan holder is uncooperative in helping the victim resolve the situation, the victim may request help from the Ombudsman at the U.S. Department of Education's Office of Federal Student Aid. Attorneys working with clients on the identity theft process may contact the Ombudsman at 202-277-3800. The Ombudsman may ask them to send notice of representation so the Ombudsman can open a case and begin working with them quickly. Attorneys also can send an inquiry via fsaombudsmanoffice@ed.gov, with confirmation of representation. The attorney will need to submit a privacy release form, which can be downloaded at www.ombudsman.ed.gov. The Ombudsman's office will work with the attorney to resolve the issues arising from the fraudulently obtained loan.

The U.S. Department of Education's Office of Inspector General (OIG) requests that victims report instances of identity theft that affect federal student aid. The OIG Hotline can be reached at 1-800-MIS-USED (1-800-647-8733) or online at www.ed.gov/misused. The OIG screens complaints for possible prosecution.

ADDITIONAL RESOURCES

The following online resources provide more information on student-loan related identity theft:

- Office of Inspector General at the U.S. Department of Education
- from the Federal Student Aid Office:
    - Avoiding Scams — online tips
    - Student Aid and Identity Theft — a PDF fact sheet
    - Save Your Money, Save Your Identity — a PDF brochure
      (or in hard copy from www.edpubs.org or 1-800-4-FED-AID)

For more information about student loan cancellation, your clients may visit www.studentaid.ed.gov/repaying and click on "Loan Discharge (Cancellation)."

Identity Theft Involving the Internal Revenue Service

An identity thief may use a victim's Social Security number to get a job or take their tax refund. Victims may receive a notice from the IRS showing payment from an unknown employer or that more than one tax return was filed in their name.

The FTC provides step-by-step guidance to address tax-related identity theft.

Identity Theft Involving the Social Security Administration

In some cases, your client may find out that the identity thief used her name and/or Social Security number (SSN) for employment purposes or for Social Security program benefits, such as Social Security Disability Insurance (SSDI) or Supplemental Security Income (SSI), or has had her Social Security checks routed to a different address or bank account. Much like financial account identity theft issues, these types of identity theft can create a unique set of problems that your client will have to address.

ERRORS ON THE VICTIM'S EARNING RECORD

Your client may find that someone has used her name and/or SSN for employment purposes when she receives a notice from the Internal Revenue Service (IRS) that he owes back taxes on income she did not report or when she receives her *Social Security Earnings Statement* and finds that the wages posted do not agree with the amount she earned. [Your client also can get a copy of her earnings record online. The Social Security Administration (SSA) has safeguards in place that minimize the effects on the victim's earnings record by verifying the name and SSN provided by the employer(s) reporting the wages and taxes before posting the earnings to the victim's record. If the SSA finds that the identity thief is working under a different name than the victim's, but using the victim's SSN, then the earnings are posted to SSA's Earnings Suspense File (ESF), instead of the victim's earnings record.

In cases where the identity thief is using both the victim's name and SSN, the erroneous earnings will be posted to the victim's earnings record and will need to be corrected not only with the SSA, but also with the IRS. The victim will need to complete IRS' Identity Theft Affidavit form. If your client suspects that someone is using her SSN for employment, or has received a notice from the IRS about unreported wages, she should contact the SSA at 1-800-772-1213, or visit her local SSA office, to speak to a representative who will assist her in correcting her Social Security records. Your client will need to provide the representative proof of her identity, including her SSN, and advise the representative about which information is incorrect. Once your client has done this, the inaccurate earnings information will be removed from her earnings record and placed into the ESF.

THEFT OF SSA BENEFITS

Much like employment-related issues, your client may find that the identity thief has used her information to gain benefits from the SSA including SSDI or SSI, or has impersonated your client to have her Social Security check sent to a different address or bank account. Your client may learn of this when she is denied benefits, a current benefit she is receiving is suspended, or when she notices that she has not received her Social Security check or deposit.

If your client finds that someone is using her SSN to obtain SSA benefits, she should go to her local SSA office and speak to a service representative, who will work with her to correct the problems with her benefits. Your client will need to bring:

- documentation to prove her identity

- a copy of a police report if she has filed one

- copies of any documentation that can help prove her allegations

- copies of past tax returns

Medical Identity Theft

Medical identity theft occurs when a thief uses a victim's name or health insurance numbers to see a doctor, get prescription drugs, file claims with an insurance provider, or get other care. If the thief's health information is mixed with the victim's, the victim's treatment, insurance and payment records, and credit report may be affected.

The FTC provides step-by-step guidance to address medical identity theft.

The "Other" Consumer Reports: "Specialty" Consumer Reports

Companies that compile reports on consumers for other than credit have been designated by Congress as "nationwide specialty consumer reporting agencies." These agencies compile reports about much more than credit history. Here are a few examples of the types of reports that they compile:

- medical conditions (e.g., the Medical Information Bureau (MIB) report)

- residential or tenant history and evictions (e.g., RentBureau)

- check writing history (e.g., ChexSystems)

- employment background checks (e.g., LexisNexis Screening Solutions)

- homeowner and auto insurance claims (e.g., CLUE reports)

The Privacy Rights Clearinghouse provides detailed information about Specialty Consumer Reports.

Appendix A:
Key Identity Theft Concepts and Tools

Identity theft is a wide-ranging topic, because the crime can take many forms, depending on how and where the individual victim's personal information is misused. Its commission and ultimate resolution usually involve many different stakeholders. Resolving a single case of identity theft may cross the boundaries of multiple statutes and legal jurisdictions. Many "terms of art" are written into the various statutes that define and provide remedies for the crime. Accordingly, this section provides a glossary of commonly used terms in identity theft issues.

Many remedies available to identity theft victims require the victim to follow specific procedures to obtain the desired benefit. Some rights are available only when certain facts are present and conditions are met. An attorney or victim may want to take a closer look at these underlying matters to be sure the required elements are present and the correct procedures have been followed, and to ascertain the specific rights to which the victim is entitled. This section provides a deeper look at key tools, including Identity Theft Reports and Affidavits, initial and extended fraud alerts, and free annual credit reports and other free credit reports.

Account fraud:

There are two basic forms of account fraud – the misuse of a victim's existing account, and the opening of a new account in the victim's name. According to FTC research, about three-fourths of identity theft victims report that the thief misused only their existing accounts. One-fourth of the victims report that the thief opened new accounts or committed other types of fraud with the victim's personal information. Credit card accounts are the most commonly misused *existing* account. Telephone accounts, usually wireless, are the most common type of *new* account opened by identity thieves. Identity thieves also open or raid bank accounts, Internet payment accounts, and auto, personal, or student loan accounts.

Blocking:

Refers to a victim's right under §605B of the Fair Credit Reporting Act to prevent information that is the result of identity theft from appearing on her credit report.

Chronic Identity Theft:

Also known as "revictimization." Occurs when a victim's identity is used more than once, often by different identity thieves, thereby forcing the victim to address repeatedly the identity theft-related problems.

Credit Report:

(Sometimes called a "Consumer Report.") A communication of any information by a credit reporting agency that bears on a consumer's credit-worthiness, credit standing, credit capacity, character, general reputation, personal characteristics, or mode of living that is used to or expected to be used to establish a consumer's eligibility for credit, insurance, employment, or other purposes. Typically refers to the reports generated by Experian, Equifax, and TransUnion. See also "Specialty Consumer Reporting Agency."

Credit Reporting Agency:

(Also known as a "CRA" Consumer Reporting Agency, and Credit Bureau.) A company that provides, assembles, and evaluates consumer credit information for the purpose of furnishing reports to third parties. Typically used to refer to Experian, Equifax, and TransUnion. But see "Specialty Consumer Reporting Agency."

Credit Freeze:

A right provided by many states that allows identity theft victims and sometimes other consumers to block the access to the consumer's credit report by potential creditors, among others. The CRAs make this right available for a fee to consumers who reside in states that do not specifically provide the right to freeze.

Criminal Identity Theft:

Criminal identity theft occurs when someone uses the victim's name and information as his own during an investigation, issuance of a ticket, or arrest by law enforcement. This may lead to the issuance of warrants or the entrance of guilty pleas in the victim's name.

Employment Identity Theft:

Some identity thieves use a victim's Social Security number for employment. Identity thieves might use another person's identity if they have a criminal record that might prevent their being hired, or if they do not have legal status to work in this country. When this happens, the employer reports income earned by the thief to the Internal Revenue Service (IRS) and the Social Security Administration (SSA) using the victim's SSN, thereby creating income tax liability for the victim, identity theft involving the IRS and identity theft involving the SSA.

Equifax:

Along with Experian and TransUnion, one of the three major nationwide credit reporting agencies.

Experian:

Along with Equifax and TransUnion, one of the three major nationwide credit reporting agencies.

Fair Credit Billing Act:

Also known as "FCBA." Federal law, codified at 15 U.S.C. §1601 *et seq.*, that provides rights and procedures that arise in relation to disputes regarding "open end" credit accounts, such as credit cards and revolving charge accounts.

Fair Credit Reporting Act:

Also known as "FCRA." Federal law, codified at 15 U.S.C. §1681 *et seq.*, which establishes rights and duties with respect to credit reporting agencies.

Fair Debt Collection Practices Act:

Also known as "FDCPA." Federal law, codified at 15 U.S.C. §§ 1692-1692p, which requires that debt collectors treat debtors fairly and prohibits certain methods of debt collection.

FCBA:

See Fair Credit Billing Act.

FCRA:

See Fair Credit Reporting Act.

FDCPA:

See Fair Debt Collection Practices Act.

Federal Trade Commission:

Federal government agency charged with enforcing various consumer protection laws and overseeing identity-theft related matters. Information on the FTC's identity theft programs at ftc.gov/idtheft.

Furnisher:

Also known as an "Information Furnisher." A creditor, debt collector, or other company that reports information about a consumer's credit payment history to a Credit Reporting Agency. For example, Joan Q. Consumer obtains a copy of her credit report from ABC Credit Bureau. The report shows that she was 30 days late in paying her XYZ credit card bill. ABC Credit Bureau is the credit reporting agency, and XYZ Credit Corp. is the furnisher of that payment information history

Fraud Alert:

An alert placed on an identity theft victim's credit report to signal to creditors and other credit report users that the consumer has reported herself as a victim of fraud or at risk of identity theft. The creditor must take reasonable steps to confirm the applicant's identity before issuing credit. Can be a 90-day alert or an extended alert that lasts for seven years.

Identity Theft Affidavit:

A document designed to help victims establish their identity with creditors and substantiate their narrative of the fraud. Victims can use the FTC Identity Theft Affidavit to dispute accounts or transactions caused by the identity theft at the institutions where the fraudulent transactions occurred.

Note: The Identity Theft Affidavit can be printed ftc.gov/idtheft, either as a blank pdf form, or as a completed form. Victims who file a complaint online with the FTC can print the Affidavit filled with most of the information they entered. The Affidavit provides space to report multiple fraudulent accounts. When disputing fraudulent accounts or transactions with a particular company, the victim should consider providing to the company only information about the relevant accounts, possibly by redacting information about other accounts. Some companies require their own affidavit of identity theft forms.

Identity Theft Report:

An official, valid law enforcement report that alleges the consumer's identity theft with specificity. It can be used to invoke certain statutory rights, including blocking identity theft-related information from appearing in the victim's credit report, preventing furnishers from continuing to furnish that information to any CRAs, preventing furnishers from selling or transferring the related debt for collection, and obtaining an extended fraud alert. An Identity Theft Report must contain sufficient detail for CRAs and information furnishers to verify the allegations of identity theft. To ensure that the Identity Theft Report contains sufficient detail, it is suggested that victims provide to law enforcement a completed Identity Theft Affidavit to attach to the police report. However, any police report containing sufficient detail can be an Identity Theft Report. For the purpose of obtaining an extended, seven-year fraud alert, which carries low risk of fraud, a completed Identity Theft Affidavit filed with the FTC and signed by the victim (but with no police involvement) provides sufficient detail.

Identity Theft Victims' Complaint and Affidavit Form:

A form available at ftc.gov/idtheft that is referred to elsewhere in this guide as the "Identity Theft Affidavit." Technically, it bears the full title, "Identity Theft Victims' Complaint and Affidavit" in recognition of its two functions: 1) when generated by the FTC's online complaint system, it is a record of the victim's complaint filed with the FTC; and, 2) it can be used as an Affidavit, *i.e.,* a voluntary statement of facts, sworn to by affirmation of the consumer signing it. The form, displaying most of the information provided in the victim's complaint, can be generated by completing the FTC Complaint Assistant, a guided interview process, or the blank form can be printed.

Medical Identity Theft:

In cases of medical identity theft, thieves use a victim's name, and possibly insurance information to obtain medical services or goods. The victim is then saddled with proving she is not responsible for costly medical bills, or may find that the thief has exhausted her insurance coverage. Even worse, medical identity theft can have serious health consequences if the thief's real or fictitious medical information is added to the victim's medical records.

Mixed File:

A credit file that has been corrupted by the inclusion of information associated with other individuals. In the case of an identity theft victim, a mixed file can result when the identity thief's application for credit provides a combination of the victim's information and someone else's information, such as using the victim's Social Security number and name, but providing his own or someone else's address, date of birth, or phone number. The victim's file can be corrupted when the creditor furnishes this mixed information to the CRA.

Mortgage Fraud:

Identity thieves can steal a victim's identity to obtain a mortgage. In an emerging form of mortgage fraud called "house stealing," thieves target an occupied home, assume the owner's identity, and have the home's deed transferred to the thief's name so that the victim no longer has ownership. NOTE: If you suspect house stealing, call the FBI immediately.

Revictimization:

Also known as "chronic identity theft," occurs when a victim's identity is used more than once, often by different identity thieves, thereby forcing the victim to repeatedly address the identity theft.

Specialty Consumer Reporting Agency:

Sometimes known as a "Specialty CRA." Company that creates consumer reports on consumer information other than credit, such as medical conditions, residential or tenant history and evictions, check writing history, employment background checks, and homeowner and auto insurance claims.

Synthetic Identity Theft:

Each of the types of identity theft listed above involves the thief impersonating the victim to obtain benefits. In some cases the thief does not steal the victim's entire identity, but rather uses only the victim's Social Security number, in combination with another person's name and birth date, to create a new, fictitious identity. As a result, the victim may experience problems when the new identity tracks back to the victim's credit or tax records. Because this type of fraud may not be reflected on a consumer's credit report, it may not be discovered by the victim for many years

Tax Fraud:

In this type of fraud, an identity thief files a tax return in the victim's name to receive a refund or other payment, such as a stimulus check. If the thief files for the refund before the victim, the IRS may deny the victim's rightful refund or stimulus check.

Trade Line:

A section of a consumer report that provides information about an account, such as when the account was opened and whether the consumer has made on-time payments on the account.

TransUnion:

Along with Experian and Equifax, one of the three major nationwide consumer reporting agencies.

Free Annual Credit Reports and Other Free Reports

Free Credit Reports

Reviewing one's credit report periodically may help spot and minimize the damage of identity theft. The Fair Credit Reporting Act (FCRA), as amended by the Fair and Accurate Credit Transactions Act (FACTA), requires each of the nationwide credit reporting agencies (CRAs) – Equifax, Experian, and TransUnion – to provide consumers with a free copy of their credit report annually, upon the consumer's request. Further, the FCRA provides victims of identity theft with the right to a free report when a fraud alert is placed on the files maintained by the CRAs. Additionally, consumers are entitled to a free report if a company takes certain adverse actions against them. These and other rights to free credit reports are discussed below.

Ordering a free annual credit report

Under the FCRA, and FTC regulations, the CRAs have set up a central website, a toll-free telephone number, and a mailing address ("authorized source") through which consumers can order their free annual reports.

To order free annual credit reports:

- visit www.annualcreditreport.com

- call 1-877-322-8228

- complete the Annual Credit Report Request Form and mail it to:
  Annual Credit Report Request Service, P.O. Box 105281, Atlanta, GA 30348-5281.

Consumers should not contact the CRAs directly to obtain their free annual credit reports. They must use the authorized source.

If a consumer requests, only the last four digits of her Social Security number will appear on the credit report that is sent.

WHEN TO ORDER REPORTS

The law allows consumers to order one free copy of their report from each of the CRAs every 12 months. FCRA § 612(a)(1)(A), 15 U.S.C. § 1681j(a)(1)(A). Consumers may order from one, two, or three of the CRAs at the same time, or they may stagger their requests. Some financial advisors say staggering requests during a 12-month period (for example, one report every four months) may be a good way to keep an eye on the accuracy and completeness of the information in the reports.

FREE TRIAL OFFERS

The CRAs and other companies advertise "free credit reports' that are bundled with the sale of other products and services (such as credit monitoring or credit scores) that the consumer may not want or need. Often, the services are offered for a free trial period, but unless the consumer cancels, she will be charged once the trial period ends. For more information about these commercial services, see "Identity Theft Protection Services."

Information consumers need to provide to get their free report

In most circumstances, the CRAs require a consumer to provide:

- name
- address
- Social Security number
- date of birth
- previous address (if she has moved in the last two years)
- answers to security questions (some information that only the consumer would know, like the amount of her monthly mortgage payment)

Each company may ask consumers for different information, because the information each has in its file may come from different sources.

If an identity thief has obtained a lease or mortgage in the victim's name, or provided another address with respect to a new credit account, the victim's file may be corrupted with the inaccurate information. In such a case, the victim's answer to the security questions may not match the information in her file, as is necessary to get a credit report from www.annualcreditreport.com. If this is the case, the victim should call or write to the CRA to obtain a copy of the report.

Timing for receipt of credit report after it has been ordered

If the consumer orders:	They receive it:
Online	Immediately
By phone	within 15 days
By mail	within 15 days

There may be times when the CRAs receive an unusually high volume of requests for credit reports. If that happens, the consumer may be asked to re-submit her request, or she may be told that her report will be mailed to her sometime after 15 days from her request. If either of these events occurs, the CRAs will let the consumer know.

Free Credit Reports Associated with Fraud Alerts

Each nationwide CRA also must provide, upon request, one free credit report to victims of identity theft who place an initial fraud alert on their file. FCRA § 605A(a)(2)(B), 15 U.S.C. § 1681c-1(a)(2)(B). Identity theft victims who obtain extended alerts are entitled to two free credit reports in the 12-month period following the placement of the alert. FCRA § 605A(b)(2)(A), 15 U.S.C. § 1681c-1(b)(2)(A). Upon the placement of such alerts, the CRAs should notify the consumer of these and other rights. The credit report(s) that a victim is entitled to receive free of charge as a result of placing a fraud alert, is in addition to, not in place of, the free annual report available by right to all consumers.

Other Rights to Free Credit Reports

IF A COMPANY TAKES ADVERSE ACTION

Under the FCRA, consumers are entitled to a free report if a company, based in whole or in part on information contained in the consumer's credit report, takes "adverse action" against the consumer, such as denying an application for credit, insurance, or employment. FCRA § 612(b), 15 U.S.C. § 1681j(b). Companies that take adverse action must provide a notice with the name, address, and phone number of the CRA for consumers to request their free report. Consumers have 60 days from their receipt of the notice to request the report.

OTHER REASONS

Consumers also are entitled to one free report a year if:

- they are unemployed and plan to look for a job within 60 days
- they believe that their credit report contains inaccurate information due to fraud (this includes all types of fraud and is not triggered by placing a fraud alert)
- they are on welfare

FCRA § 612(c), 15 U.S.C. § 1681j(c)

HOW TO REQUEST

Instructions on how to obtain a free or reduced-fee credit report for each of these reasons appears on the websites of the three CRAs. If a consumer wishes to order an additional credit report beyond those she can obtain for free, the CRA may charge up to $11.00 for the additional report. Some states have passed laws that allow a consumer to receive a free credit report from each of the CRAs every 12 months in addition to their free annual credit report.

To obtain a copy of their report, other than their free annual reports, consumers may contact:

Equifax: 800-685-1111; www.equifax.com

Experian: 888-EXPERIAN (888-397-3742); www.experian.com

TransUnion: 800-916-8800; www.transunion.com

Specialty Consumer Reports

In addition to the three nationwide CRAs, there are numerous CRAs that compile and sell consumer information for non-credit related purposes, such as employment, real property rental, and insurance. The information may relate to the consumer's medical condition, rental or employment history, or insurance claims. The FCRA gives consumers rights with respect to these "specialty CRAs" if they operate on a nationwide basis.

The FCRA entitles consumers to a free annual report from nationwide specialty CRAs. There is no central source for obtaining the reports, however; consumers must contact each agency. If your client has been the victim of non-financial account identity theft, such as medical identity theft, Social Security number misuse, employment, or rental identity theft, it is suggested she obtain copies of these reports.

Proof of Identity

Establishing One's Identity

An identity theft victim will have to establish "proof of identity" to exercise certain rights under the Fair Credit Reporting Act (FCRA). There are two different standards, depending on what rights the consumer is seeking to exercise:

1. for a victim to obtain documentation from a business about its transactions with the person who stole her identity, the victim must be able to verify her identity to the business
2. credit reporting agencies (CRAs) also must verify an identity theft victim's identity to provide the victim with certain statutory rights

The Tools for Establishing Identity
BUSINESS RECORDS
Before a business provides any documentation to an alleged identity theft victim, it must:

- have a high degree of confidence that it knows the identity of the alleged victim making the document request or
- obtain positive identification from the victim

Indeed, if the business lacks the requisite "high degree of confidence," or other positive evidence of the victim's identity, it may decline the victim's information request. FCRA § 609(e), 15 U.S.C. § 1681g(e).

When seeking transaction records related to identity theft, an identity theft victim may establish positive identification in one of three ways, at the election of the business entity, under section 609(e)(2)(A) of the FCRA.

3. the victim may be asked to present a government-issued identification card
4. the victim may be asked to present personally identifying information of the same type as was provided to the business by the unauthorized person
5. the business may ask the victim to provide the type of personally identifying information the business entity typically requests from new applicants or for new transactions. Personally identifying information may include the victim's Social Security number and copies of financial records, recent tax return, or similar records

CREDIT REPORTING AGENCIES
Credit reporting agencies (CRAs) may ask a consumer to provide proof of identity to:

- block fraudulent information from appearing on her credit reports

- provide the consumer with her credit report
- place a 7-year fraud alert

CRAs must develop and implement reasonable requirements for what will be acceptable proof of identity.

While CRAs have flexibility in determining what constitutes proof of identity, the FTC's Appropriate Proof of Identity Rule, 16 C.F.R. § 614, provides the following guidance:

1. CRAs must ensure the information they ask an identity theft victim to furnish is "sufficient to enable the CRA to match consumers with their files"

2. the information must be "commensurate with an identifiable risk of harm arising from misidentifying the consumer"

Reasonable information requirements necessary to match the consumer with her files includethe consumer's full name (first, middle initial, last, suffix), any other or previously used names, current and/or recent full address (street number and name, apartment number, city, state, and zip code), full Social Security number, and/or date of birth.

Additional items of proof of identity may include copies of government issued identification documents and utility bills. Consumers also may be asked to verify their identity by answering verification questions to which only they might be expected to know the answer.

Authorization Form for Attorneys

AUTHORIZATION TO_____

Name:

Address:

DOB:

SSN:

Prior Address:

I authorize _____ to provide ___[insert attorney's name, attorney's company's name, if appropriate, and attorney's relationship to signatory]__ all of the following documents in your possession:

Applications for Credit	Monthly Statements
Adverse Action Notices	Correspondence (of any kind)
Universal Data Forms (UDF)	Automated Universal Data Forms (AUDF)
Requests for Investigations of Credit Data	Results of Investigations of Credit Data
Consumer Dispute Verification Forms (CDV)	Credit Reports
Payments/Payment History	Account Reviews
Automated Consumer Dispute Verification Forms	Credit Denial Determinations

for the following accounts:

1.

2.

I also authorize _____ to directly discuss the above account(s) with _____[insert attorney's name and, if appropriate, attorney's company's name]___. This authorization shall expire on _____.

YOU MAY ACCEPT A COPY OF THIS DOCUMENT IN LIEU OF THE ORIGINAL.

_____

_____

Signature

County/City of _____

State of _____.

On this _____ day of _____, 2011, _____ personally appeared before me and acknowledged that he/she executed the foregoing instrument.

_____

Notary Public

My commission expires on _____

Online Resources for Attorneys and Victim Service Providers

Consumer Organizations

- Identity Theft Resource Center – www.idtheftcenter.org
- Maryland Crime Victims' Resource Center – www.mdcrimevictims.org
- SAFE - Stop Atlanta Fraud Empower – www.atlantava.org
- Victims Initiative for Counseling, Advocacy, and Restoration of the Southwest (VICARS) www.idvictim.org
- Call for Action – www.callforaction.org
- Consumer Credit Counseling Service of Orange County – www.cccsoc.org/index.phtml

- Identity Theft Prevention and Survival – www.identitytheft.org
- Law Help – www.lawhelp.org
- National Consumers League – www.nclnet.org
- Privacy Rights Clearinghouse – www.privacyrights.org/identity.htm

Federal and State Government

- Federal Trade Commission – www.ftc.gov/idtheft
- California Office of Privacy Protection – www.privacy.ca.gov
- Internal Revenue Service – www.irs.gov/privacy/article/0,,id=186436,00.html
- Internet Crime Complaint Center – www.ic3.gov
- National Conference of State Legislatures www.ncsl.org//Default.aspx?TabID=756&tabs=951,60,472#951
- National Criminal Justice Reference Service – www.ncjrs.gov/spotlight/identity_theft/programs.html
- OnGuardOnline – www.onguardonline.gov/
- Social Security Administration – www.ssa.gov/pubs/10064.html
- U.S. Department of Justice – www.usdoj.gov/criminal/fraud/websites/idtheft.html
    - Office for Victims of Crime – http://www.ojp.usdoj.gov/ovc/help/index.html
    - OVC Training and Technical Assistance Center - www.ovcttac.gov
- U.S. Postal Inspection Service – postalinspectors.uspis.gov
- U.S. Bankruptcy Trustee Program – www.usdoj.gov/ust

Professional Associations

- AARP – www.aarp.org
- Identity Theft Assistance Center – www.identitytheftassistance.org
- International Association of Chiefs of Police – www.idsafety.org
- Law Library Resource Xchange - www.llrx.com/features/idtheft.htm
- National Consumer Law Center - www.consumerlaw.org
- Probono.net – www.probono.net

Appendix B: Checklists

An attorney or victim advocate needs to gain a comprehensive understanding of the facts surrounding an identity theft victim's situation to ascertain what legal rights their client may need to invoke during their recovery. A list of questions that you can use during the intake interview to draw out the details of your client's situation is in this section.

The steps that a victim must take to respond effectively to identity theft can be complicated, depending on how the victim's personal information has been used and how cooperative the various parties involved in the recovery may be. A checklist of the initial steps most identity theft victims need to take to stop further harm, determine the scope of the crime, and begin the recovery process in this section, too. It is intended for situations that involve more than the misuse of a victim's existing credit cards.

This section also has checklists to guide your client through the procedures she needs to follow to exercise her section 605B blocking rights with credit reporting agencies and information furnishers, and to exercise her rights with respect to debt collectors.

List of Sample Questions for Intake Interview

This chart has a list of questions to help you understand your client's situation, particularly if you need to follow up on an incident that your client mentioned only briefly . The third column indicates which sections of this Guide are likely to apply to the situations listed. Thanks to the Identity Theft Resource Center (www.idtheftcenter.org) for allowing use of its Victim Intake Questionnaire as the basis for this chart.

Category	Question	Page/Location
Financial	Were any new credit cards or revolving charge cards opened in your name or using your information?	29 or 32
Credit Cards	Were any of your existing credit cards or revolving charge cards used?	34
	Do you still have them in your possession or were they stolen?	
	If they are still in your possession, do you know how the thief obtained the account number(s)?	
	Did you receive a breach notification letter?	
ATM Cards	Were any of your ATM or debit cards used?	32
	Do you still have them in your possession or were they stolen?	
	If they are still in your possession, do you know how the thief obtained the account and PIN number(s)?	
	Did you receive a breach notification letter from a financial institution?	
Checks	Were any checks written using any part of your information?	31 and Privacyrights.org
	What part of your information was used (name, address, phone number, account and routing number)?	
	Had your checks been lost or stolen?	
	Were any checks written using your information but using a different account and routing number then your own?	
	Were any new checking accounts opened in your name or using your information?	
Loans	Have any personal, car, or house loans been obtained using your information?	29 or 31

	Have any student loans been obtained?	43 or 29 or 32
	Have any funds from your own student loan been diverted to an account other than your own?	
	Have any charges been made to your existing wireless account or has a new wireless phone account been opened in your name?	36 or 29 or 32
	What about any landline accounts?	
	Have any charges been made to your existing cable, satellite, electricity, gas, or other utility accounts? Has anyone opened any such new utility accounts in your name?	
	Has anyone opened a specialty credit card, such as a gasoline credit cart, in your name?	
	Have you had any problems with someone misusing your existing Internet access account, or any of your Internet-based payment accounts such as Paypal, or any email or social network account?	36 or 29 or 32
	Has anyone opened any new internet related accounts in your name?	
	Have any collection agencies contacted you regarding a past due bill? Have any of your existing accounts been reported to debt collectors?	38
Medical	Have you received a bill for any medical care you didn't receive?	Consumer.ftc.gov
	Have you received an explanation of benefits from your insurance company for an office visit, medical treatment, or medications you did not have or obtain?	or 29 or 32
	Have you received information from a health insurance company for a policy that you didn't obtain?	
Employment	Has someone been working using your information?	IRS.gov, 45
	How did you find out?	or 29 or 32
	Has it impacted your tax, Social Security or unemployment benefits situation?	

63

Tax	Were you notified of a problem by the IRS?	IRS.gov, 45
	Did they keep part of your refund or ask for more money because you didn't declare a job or were not entitled to one of the exemptions?	
	Did they withhold your refund because someone had already claimed it in your name?	
Benefits	Were you denied benefits such as Medicare, disability, welfare, unemployment, health benefits, social service, disaster relief or SS benefits?	45, Consumer.ftc.gov
	Did they keep part of your refund/payment because you didn't declare a job?	
Driver's License	If the suspect bought a car, he may have used a driver's license (DL) or state issued identification card. Request a copy of the purchase/loan paperwork and then contact the state where the DL or State ID used was issued and where the car was bought.	40
	You may need to ask to have the DL or State ID revoked. In some instances, the DL or ID that was used was forged and there is no corresponding information from the state that is available.	
	You also should ask the state to run a criminal background check to verify that the thief didn't use the DL or State ID when being ticketed or arrested for another crime.	
Housing, Lease	Has your application to rent and apartment or house been refused?	46 and Privacyrights.org
	Have you been contacted by a collection agency regarding past due rental fees?	
	Does a hard inquiry from a landlord or rental company appear on your credit report?	
Family/Child	Do you know who the identity thief is, and if so, how? Did anyone you know have access to your information?	If child: consumer.ftc.gov
	Do you have proof other than hearsay?	
	What do you want to do about this situation? How do you feel about filing a police report? Do you know what your options are?	

Criminal	How did you find out that someone had created a criminal record in your name or using your information?	Privacyrights.org
	Who have you spoken with? Is there booking information on the original person to compare with your information (for example, a picture or fingerprints)?	
	If outstanding warrants exist: Have you determined where the warrants are from? Did you call the court clerk to find out what the warrants are for and what agency issued the warrant?	
	If the victim is calling from jail: Have the police compared fingerprints or booking information with the jurisdiction that ordered the arrest?	

Checklist for General Steps Addressing Identity Theft

This checklist walks through the steps the victim should take to preserve her rights, minimize further harm, and begin to restore her identity. Use this checklist during the initial interview to identify what steps your client has taken herself so you can chart the steps that remain, or to make sure you have taken all appropriate steps to address your client's particular problems.

Steps to Take with the Credit Reporting Agencies

- Placing Fraud Alerts

- Obtaining and Reviewing Credit Reports

- Fixing the Reports

Placing Fraud Alerts

❑ Contact the credit reporting agencies (CRAs) to place an initial 90-day fraud alert and consider a credit freeze.)

- Issues to consider:

    - Consider placing an extended 7-year fraud alert or a credit freeze on the report immediately.

    - For certain types of identity theft, e.g., employment or housing-related, the victim may need to contact specialty CRAs. Specialty CRAs are not required by the Fair Credit Reporting Act (FCRA) to provide fraud alerts. However, they are required to provide a free annual report, although there is no central source for ordering such reports. Requests must be made directly to each specialty CRAs.

❑ Confirm that the victim has received letters from all 3 major CRAs confirming that they have successfully placed the 90-day fraud alert.

- Note: If the victim did not receive a confirmation letter from any one of the three major CRAs, she should contact that company directly to place a fraud alert, and may be asked to provide the company with additional proof of identity. It may be that the information the victim initially provided to the CRA does not match the information in her credit file.

Obtaining and Reviewing Credit Reports

❑ Order and receive her free credit reports from all three CRAs.

- The CRAs' fraud alert confirmation letters will instruct the victim how to get the free credit reports she is entitled to following the placement of a fraud alert.

    - These reports must be provided free of charge, and the victim is not required to buy any additional product or service to obtain these free reports.

❑ Review the credit report(s) for errors related to the theft of her identity and dispute any errors.

❑ If the victim detects identity theft-related errors on any of her credit reports, she can block the information from appearing in her credit reports by submitting an Identity Theft Report to the appropriate CRAs.

  • Note: Ask the CRA for the specific address (if any) to which the Identity Theft Report and blocking request should be sent.

❑ Respond to any requests by a CRA to supply additional information in response to the Identity Theft Report.

  • The CRAs may ask for additional supporting information in some cases.

❑ Obtain a follow-up credit report from each of the three CRAs within a few weeks after sending the blocking request and Identity Theft Report (or after sending additional information requested) to verify that the information she challenged was indeed blocked.

❑ If the victim did not obtain an Identity Theft Report from law enforcement, or wants corrected information to appear on her credit report (such as where the identity theft affected an existing account and the victim wants the correct information about the account to continue to appear on her credit report), she can dispute the erroneous information in the credit reports using FCRA section 611.

❑ Confirm receipt of a notice from the CRAs reporting the results of their investigation under section 611.

  • The victim should provide written disputes to the CRAs before or when she writes the furnishers to inform them of the fraud.

  • All disputes should be sent by certified mail, return receipt requested.

Steps to Take With Creditors

  • Contacting Companies and Repairing Damage

  • Obtaining Documents

  • Obtaining Release Letters

❑ Telephone the fraud departments at each of the companies where new accounts were opened, or where her existing accounts were used without her knowledge or permission. Notify them of the identity theft and request that the account be closed or frozen immediately while she disputes the fraudulent activity.

  • Ask the company if it accepts the FTC Identity Theft Affidavit or if it has a particular form that it requires for disputing the accounts or transactions resulting from identity theft.

- Ask the company for the specific address to which the dispute letter (or, if applicable, the Identity Theft Report) should be sent.

❑ Mail the company a follow-up letter identifying the identity theft-related activity, accompanied by an Identity Theft Affidavit or Report and proof of identity. The letter should ask the company to close the account, absolve the victim of all associated debts, cease reporting the fraudulent activity to the CRAs, and not sell or transfer the disputed debt. All disputes should be sent by certified mail, return receipt requested.

❑ Change passwords on all existing accounts.

Obtaining Documents

❑ Request that the companies provide all documents underlying the fraudulent transactions, as provided under section 609(e) of the FCRA.

- Ask the company if there is a specific address to which this document request should be sent.

Obtaining Release Letters

❑ Request a letter from each company stating that the company has closed the disputed account(s) and has discharged the fraudulent debts.

- Confirm that each company provided a discharge letter.

Using Resources from the Federal Trade Commission

- Filing a Complaint
- Obtaining a Printed Identity Theft Affidavit

Filing a Complaint

❑ Before filing a complaint with the FTC, compile all possible documentation regarding the details of the crime.

- Note: Assemble credit reports and all relevant business documents, including bills or dunning notices for debts that the thief incurred, merchandise or payment cards ordered by the thief that were shipped to the victim's home, and any information about any other unusual uses of the victim's personal information.

❑ Review the credit reports and other documentation for information about the misuse of her identity.

- The FTC complaint asks for:

  - information that would help identify the thief (name, mailing address, telephone number, etc.,)

  - the estimated date her personal information was stolen

- the name of each company or institution where the thief committed fraud using her personal information, the type of account or transaction involved, and the relevant account or transaction number(s), if any

- relevant dates for loss of data, misuse by the thief, or other events

- the estimated value of what the thief obtained by using her information at each institution or entity

- erroneous changes or additions to her personal information, such a new address being added

- inquiries on her credit report from potential creditors, insurers, employers, landlords, or others for suspect transactions

Obtaining a Printed Identity Theft Affidavit

Where new accounts have been opened in the victim's name, an FTC ID Theft Affidavit is accepted by many companies to prove that the victim did not open the account and is not responsible for the debt. Some companies, however, require the victim to use that company's own Affidavit. The victim should check with each company to see if it accepts the FTC Affidavit when she calls the company.

❑ To create an FTC Affidavit with most of the information filled in, enter the relevant information online through the FTC's Complaint Assistant and print a copy. (It will be printed as an Identity Theft Affidavit.)

- If your client does not have access to a computer, help her complete the online form at your office.

- **Important Note:** You must print the complaint as soon as you complete it. The document cannot be saved and printed at a later time. Therefore, be sure that a printer is connected to the computer. Complaints phoned in to the FTC ID Theft Hotline cannot be printed out and mailed to the victim. You also can download and print a blank copy of the ID Theft Affidavit.

Law Enforcement

- Filing a Report

- Obtaining an Identity Theft Report

Filing a Report

❑ Contact the police by phone to make an initial report of the crime.

- Note: The victim should offer to provide any information about the crime that the police want at that time.

❑ Tell the officer that she needs to obtain a copy of the official police report containing as much detail as possible about the crime. Make an appointment to come to the station in-person to file and get a copy of the official police report.

- Note: The appointment should be set for a time by which the victim will have obtained and reviewed her credit reports and gathered her documentation. These documents will help the victim present the full extent of the crime.

❑ Assemble a file to take to the police, containing copies of the following documents, where possible:

- a completed Identity Theft Affidavit Form

- an Action Log

- credit reports (at least one) and any other documents related to the misuse of her identity

- proof of her identity such as a government-issued ID card and

- proof of her residency at the time the thief misused her information, such as a bank statement or utility bill

Obtaining an Official Police Report That Can Be Used as an Identity Theft Report

❑ Meet in-person with the police to file the detailed police report.

- Have the police officer sign the victim's Identity Theft Affidavit and attach it to the Official Police Report.

- If the police will not include the Affidavit with their official report, ensure that the Official Police Report contains sufficient detail to verify the victim's allegations of the crime, such as institution names and account numbers, dates related to the theft and misuse of the victim's identity, and information the victim might have about the identity of the thief.

❑ Obtain a copy of the Official Police Report.

- Note: The victim may wish to bring a copy of the FTC *Staff Memorandum to Police on the Importance of Taking Identity Theft Police Reports*. The victim also may want give the police a copy of the sample letter for law enforcement to use as a cover letter to obtain identity theft-related documents from companies without a subpoena under section 609(e) of the FCRA.

Checklist - Blocking Fraudulent Information from Credit Reports, Credit Reporting Agencies' Obligations under FCRA Section 605B

This checklist can help you determine whether all appropriate steps have been taken to invoke your client's rights under the Fair Credit Reporting Act (FCRA) to block identity theft-related debts and inaccurate information from appearing as trade lines on her credit reports at the three nationwide credit reporting agencies (CRAs). The key to success is providing a satisfactory Identity Theft Report so that no additional information will be requested by the CRA. There are certain requirements that must be met by the victim to trigger the CRAs' obligations. Likewise, the CRAs' obligations must be met within certain standards and timeframes.

How to Initiate a 605B Request

Legal Standards for an Identity Theft Report

- a copy of an official valid report filed by the victim with a law enforcement agency

- exposes the victim to criminal penalties relating to the filing of the false information

- alleges identity theft with as much specificity as the victim can provide

- may include additional information that an information furnisher or credit reporting agency may reasonably request to determine the validity of the allegations

16 C.F.R. § 603.3(a)

The 605B Package Documentation Requirements

❑ a letter requesting that the fraudulent information resulting from identity theft be blocked from appearing in her credit report. The letter should include a victim's statement that the information does not relate to any transaction she made

❑ a copy of the victim's Identity Theft Report

❑ identification of the fraudulent information (usually provided in the Identity Theft Report as well as in a marked-up copy of the victim's credit report)

❑ proof of the victim's identity.

FCRA § 605B(a)

The Legal Standard for Specificity of Allegations

As much detail as the victim knows about the identity theft, e.g.:

- dates relating to when the theft of the victim's personally identifying information occurred and when the fraud(s) using the victim's personal information occurred;

- information the victim knows about the perpetrator; and

- account information related to the identity theft, such as names of companies where accounts were opened or accessed by the identity thieves, and the related account numbers.

16 C.F.R. § 603.3(b)

Legal Standard and Timing Requirements for Requesting Additional Information

The Legal Standard for the CRA to Request Additional Information

- the CRA must reasonably determine that the Identity Theft Report does not contain enough detail for it to verify the alleged identity theft

- the CRA must allow the victim an opportunity to remedy the lack of specific information by requesting additional information and documentation from the victim

16 C.F.R. § 603.3(a)(3)

Timeframe for Requesting Additional Information

- initial requests for additional information must be made within 15 days of receiving the victim's Identity Theft Report

- second requests for information must be made within another 15 days of its first request for information

- the decision regarding acceptance of the Identity Theft Report must be made within 15 days of its initial request, or within 5 days of receiving the requested additional information, if the CRA receives the requested information between the 11th and 15th day of the second 15-day period

16 C.F.R. § 603.3(a)(3)(i)-(iii)

Legal Standard and Notification Requirements for Refusing to Place a Block

Legal Standard for CRA to Refuse to Place a Block

- must "reasonably determine" that one of the following circumstances exists:

  - the victim made a material misrepresentation of fact relevant to the block request

  - the victim erroneously requested the block, or

  - the victim acquired goods, services or money as a result of the transaction(s) identified as fraudulent in the blocking request

FCRA § 605B(c)

CRA's Notification Requirements upon Refusing to Place a Block

- must notify the victim of its decision to refuse to place the block and the specific reason for the decision within five business days

FCRA § 605B(c)(2)

Requirements Upon Accepting Identity Theft Report

Timeframe for Placing Block upon Accepting the Identity Theft Report

- must block the fraudulent information within four business days

FCRA § 605B(a)

Notification to Furnishers

- must promptly notify the furnisher of the information identified as fraudulent of the following:

    - that the information may have resulted from identity theft

    - that an Identity Theft Report has been filed

    - that a block has been requested under this section, and

    - the effective dates of the block

FCRA § 605B(b)

Notification to Victim

- **Note:** There is no requirement under FCRA section 605B(b) that a CRA inform the victim when it accepts the Identity Theft Report, places the block, and notifies the furnisher that it has accepted the victim's Identity Theft Report.

- Best practice would be that the CRA provide such notification to the victim.

Follow up Best Practices for Victims

Verification of Information Blocking by CRA

❑ Order a copy of the victim's credit report two weeks after sending the CRA the victim's blocking request.

❑ If the information has not been blocked, the attorney should review the Identity Theft Report to make sure it meets the relevant criteria, and if so, contact the CRA for an explanation.

Verification of Notification to Furnishers and Furnisher's Compliance

❑ Order a copy of the victim's credit report two weeks after sending the CRA the victim's blocking request.

❑ If the fraudulent information reappears on the victim's credit report, or the fraudulent debt is sold to another party for collection, follow up with an inquiry to the CRA and to the information furnisher to determine the cause.

Checklist - Debt Collectors' Obligations under FCRA Sections 615(f), (g) and FDCPA Sections 805(c), 809(b)

This checklist can help you determine whether your client has taken all the necessary steps to invoke the protections covering debt collectors provided by the Fair Credit Reporting Act (FCRA) and the Fair Debt Collection Practices Act (FDCPA). The FCRA requires that a debt collector, in its role as an information furnisher (the business that sent the disputed information to the credit reporting agency (CRA)) must stop reporting the blocked information to any CRA, and may not sell, transfer for consideration, or place for collection any debt relating to the victim's blocking request once it has been notified by a CRA that it has accepted a victim's Identity Theft Report. Further, under the FCRA, when the victim or a CRA notifies the debt collector of the identity theft, the collector must notify the initial creditor that the debt may be fraudulent, and, upon the request of the victim, provide the victim with information about the underlying suspect transaction, as they otherwise would be entitled under the FDCPA.

Under the FDCPA, consumers, including identity theft victims, can stop a debt collector from further contacts by writing a letter telling it to stop. In addition, a debt collector must suspend collection efforts until it has given to the consumer written verification if the consumer has disputed the debt in writing within 30 days of being notified of this right.

Steps to Take with the Debt Collection Agencies

Contact the Debt Collector and CRAs

❑ Report to both entities that the fraudulent debt is the result of identity theft

❑ Follow up in writing with both entities

❑ Send the debt collector the written dispute within the 30 day period

❑ Send the debt collector a letter telling the collector to stop contacting the victim about the debt and

❑ Request documentation from the debtor collector pertaining to the account or transaction

Obligations of Debt Collection Agencies Upon Written Notification

❑ Must send the victim written verification of the debt, or, stop attempting to collect on the debt;

❑ Must not continue to contact the victim, and

❑ Must notify the initial creditor that the debt may be fraudulent.

Steps to Take if the CRAs or Debt Collectors do Not Meet Their Obligations

If the CRA has not notified the debt collector that the debt is the result of identity theft:

❑ send a follow-up letter to remind the CRA of its duties to report under section 605B of the FCRA.

If the debt collector attempts to sell, transfer, or place the debt for collection:

❑ send a follow-up letter to remind the debt collector of its obligation (upon notification by the CRA) under section 615(f)(1) of the FCRA, to cease selling, transferring, or placing the debt for collection.

If the debt collector has not stopped attempting to collect on the debt:

❑ send a follow-up letter to remind the debt collector that under section 809(b) of the FDCPA, it must cease collection attempts until the collector has mailed the victim written verification of the debt.

If the debt collector has not stopped contacting the consumer about the debt:

❑ send a follow-up letter to remind the collector that under section 805(c) of the FDCPA it must cease contacting the victim.

If the consumer was unsuccessful in obtaining documentation:

❑ send a follow-up letter to the debt collector reminding them of their obligation to furnish documentation under section 615(g) of the FCRA.

Appendix C: Sample Letters

Drafting effective dispute letters can be a new and challenging process for some consumers. This section includes sample letters that victims can use to dispute fraudulent charges, request changes to their credit reports, and take other steps to restore their identities. Because consumer letters do not always resolve the disputes, this section also includes sample attorney follow-up letters. The letters use a format that can be tailored to the facts of your client's case.

Although each of the letters in this section focuses on a single issue and the relevant laws that address just that issue, some victims have multiple issues; you may choose to use a single letter to address multiple issues. Note also that these letters are designed to resolve the consumer dispute directly with the business or other entity. They do not threaten a legal action on your client's behalf. You may wish to change the approach if you determine that litigation may be necessary in a given circumstance.

Blocking Request Letters Under §§ 605B and 623(a)(6)(B)

Your clients can use the following letters to contact credit reporting agencies (CRAs) and companies that have furnished information about your client to the CRAs to request that they block all inaccurate information resulting from identity theft from appearing on your client's credit reports.

- Consumer 605B Blocking Request Letter to Credit Reporting Agencies
- Attorney 605B Blocking Follow-up Letter to Credit Reporting Agencies
- Consumer 623(a)(6)(B) Blocking Letter to Information Furnisher – Existing Accounts
- Consumer 623(a)(6)(B) Blocking Letter to Information Furnisher – New Accounts
- Attorney 605B and 623(a)(6)(B) Blocking Letter for Information Furnishers

Consumer § 605B Blocking Request Letter to CRA

[Date]

[Your Name]
[Your Address]
[Your City, State, Zip Code]

(Write to each relevant credit reporting agency, one at a time:)

Equifax Consumer Fraud Division
P.O. Box 740256
Atlanta, GA 30374

-or-

Experian
P.O. Box 9532
Allen, TX 75013

-or-

TransUnion
Fraud Victim Assistance Department
P.O. Box 6790
Fullerton, CA 92834-6790

[RE: Your Account Number (if known)]

Dear Sir or Madam:

I am a victim of identity theft. The information listed below, which appears on my credit report, does not relate to any transaction(s) that I have made. It is the result of identity theft.

[Identify item(s) resulting from the identity theft that should be blocked, by name of the source, such as the credit card issuer or bank, and type of item, such as credit account, checking account, etc.]

Please block this information from my credit report, pursuant to section 605B of the Fair Credit Reporting Act, and send the required notifications to all furnishers of this information.

Enclosed are the following:

- A copy of my credit report I received from your company. The fraudulent items are circled.

- A copy of my Identity Theft Report and proof of my identity.

- A copy of section 605B of the Fair Credit Reporting Act, which requires you to block the fraudulent information on my credit report resulting from identity theft within four business days and to promptly notify the furnisher(s) of that information.

I appreciate your prompt attention to this matter, and await your reply.

Sincerely,
[Your Name]

Enclosures: [List what you are enclosing]

- Copy of Credit Report
- Identity Theft Report
- Proof of Identity
- FCRA § 605B, 15 U.S.C. § 1681c-2

Attorney § 605B Blocking Request Letter to CRA

[Date]

[Attorney's Name and Company Heading]
(Write to each relevant credit reporting agency, one at a time:)

Equifax Consumer Fraud Division
P.O. Box 740256
Atlanta, GA 30374

     -or-

Experian
P.O. Box 9532
Allen, TX 75013

     -or-

TransUnion
Fraud Victim Assistance Department
P.O. Box 6790
Fullerton, CA 92834-6790

RE: [Your Identity Theft Client's Name]
       [Your Client's Account Number, if Applicable]

Dear Sir or Madam:

I write on behalf of my client, [Client's Name], concerning [his/her] request that you block fraudulent information resulting from identity theft from [his/her] credit report, as required by section 605B of the Fair Credit Reporting Act.

This letter follows an earlier request made to you by my client. [He/she] requested the block in a letter to you dated [insert date], accompanied by an Identity Theft Report and proof of [his/her] identity. [If possible: Enclosed for your reference is a copy of that letter and attachments thereto]. My client reports that [summarize the nature of the problem with the credit reporting agency's (CRA) response]. Examples:

Scenario 1: [Company's Name] refused [Client's Name] blocking request, stating that [his/her] Identity Theft Report did not contain sufficient detail. However, your company has made no request for additional information or documentation to assist it in verifying my client's allegations of identity theft.

     -or

Scenario 2: [Company's Name] declined [Client's Name] blocking request but [did not give a reason for the decision] or [did not notify my client of its decision].

A CRA such as [Company's Name] is required to block fraudulent information from appearing on a consumer=s credit report within four business days of receiving the request if the consumer sends them a copy of an Identity Theft Report, appropriate proof of the consumer's identity, and a letter stating that the information does not relate to any transaction that the consumer made or authorized. Fair Credit Reporting Act (FCRA) § 605B(a), 15 U.S.C. §1681c-2(a).

Notwithstanding the requirements of the FCRA, it appears that [Company's Name]'s [insert description of company's response] does not comply with the requirements of the FCRA. Under the FCRA, [insert a brief statement as to why it does not appear to comply]. Examples:

Scenario 1: While a CRA may decline to accept a consumer's Identity Theft Report if it does not contain enough detail for the company to verify the alleged identity theft, (16 C.F.R. Part 603.3(a)(3)), if it does so, the company must request additional information from the consumer within 15 days of receiving the consumer's blocking request. The company can make a second request within another 15 days of its first request for information. 16 C.F.R. Part 603.3(a)(3)(i) B (iii).

Scenario 2: Where the consumer has provided a complete blocking request and Identity Theft Report, the CRA can refuse to block the information that is identified as inaccurate as a result of identity theft in the consumer's blocking request only if the company has a reasonable basis for determining that one of the three following circumstances exists:

1. the consumer made a material misrepresentation of fact relevant to the blocking request; or

2. the consumer acquired goods, services, or money as a result of the transactions identified as fraudulent in the blocking request; or

3. the consumer erroneously requested the block.

FCRA § 605B(c)(1), 15 U.S.C. §1681c-2(c)(1).

If the CRA refuses to block the information for any of the three reasons listed above, it must notify the consumer of this decision and the specific reason for the decision within five business days. FCRA § 605B(c)(2), 15 U.S.C. §1681c-2(c)(2).

Scenario 3: If the CRA refuses to block the information, under no circumstances may the CRA convert the consumer's blocking request to a reinvestigation request under section

611 of the FCRA. It must notify the consumer of its decision to refuse to block the information and the specific reason for the decision within five business days. FCRA § 605B(c)(2), 15 U.S.C. §1681c-2(c)(2). Otherwise, the CRA must block the fraudulent information within four business days of receiving the blocking request. FCRA § 605B(a), 15 U.S.C. §1681c-2(a). Moreover, it is the responsibility of the CRA to promptly notify the companies that furnished the disputed information that the information may be a result of identity theft, that the consumer filed an Identity Theft Report, that a block has been requested under section 605B, and the effective dates of the block. FCRA § 605B(b), 15 U.S.C. §1681c-2(b).

I look forward to hearing from you and resolving this matter quickly. Please telephone or provide a written explanation within 14 days of the date of this letter. I can be reached at [insert phone number].

Sincerely,
[Attorney's Name]

Enclosures:

- **Letter from** [Client's Name] **to** [Credit Reporting Agency's Name] **dated** [insert date]
- **Identity Theft Report of** [Client's Name]
- **Proof of Identity of** [Client's Name]
- **FCRA § 605B, 15 U.S.C. § 1681c-2**

Consumer §§ 605B and 623(a)(6)(B) Dispute Letter for Furnishers re: Existing Accounts (Note: Consumer may also have FCBA remedies)

[Date]

[Your Name]
[Your Address]
[Your City, State, Zip Code]

[Name of Company]
[Fraud Department (companies may specify an address to receive fraud dispute letters), or Billing Inquiries Department]
[Address]
[City, State, Zip Code]

[RE: Your Account Number (if known)]

Dear Sir or Madam:

I am writing to dispute [a] fraudulent charge(s) on my account in the amount(s) of $____, and posted on [dates]. I am a victim of identity theft, and I did not make [this/these] charge(s). I request that you remove the fraudulent charge(s) and any related finance charge and other charges from my account, send me an updated and accurate statement, and close the account (if applicable). I also request that you cease reporting the inaccurate information to all of the nationwide credit reporting agencies (CRAs) to which you provided it.

Enclosed is a copy of my Identity Theft Report supporting my position, and a copy of my credit report showing the fraudulent items related to your company that are the result of identity theft. [Consumers should redact information that is unrelated to the dispute with this company.] Also enclosed is a copy of the Notice to Furnishers issued by the Federal Trade Commission, which details your responsibilities under the Fair Credit Reporting Act as an information furnisher to CRAs. The Notice also specifies your responsibilities when you receive notice from a CRA, under section 605B of the Fair Credit Reporting Act, that information you provided to the CRA may be the result of identity theft. Those responsibilities include ceasing to provide the inaccurate information to any CRAs, and ensuring that you do not attempt to sell or transfer the fraudulent debts to another party for collection.

Please investigate this matter and send me a written explanation of your findings and actions.

Sincerely,
[Your Name]

Enclosures: [List what you are enclosing]

- Proof of identity
- Identity Theft Report

- Credit report of [Consumer's Name] identifying information not to be reported or to be Corrected

- FTC Notice to Furnishers of Information

Consumer §§ 605B and 623(a)(6)(B) Dispute Letter for Furnishers re: New Accounts

[Date]

[Your Name]
[Your Address]
[Your City, State, Zip Code]

[Name of Company]
[Fraud Department (companies may specify an address to receive fraud dispute letters),
orBilling Inquiries Department]
[Address]
[City, State, Zip Code]

[RE: Your Account Number (if known)]

Dear Sir or Madam:

I am a victim of identity theft. I recently learned that my personal information was used to open an account at your company. I did not open or authorize this account, and I therefore request that it be closed immediately. I also request that [Company Name] absolve me of all charges on the account, and that you take all appropriate steps to remove information about this account from my credit files.

Enclosed is a copy of my Identity Theft Report supporting my position, and a copy of my credit report showing the fraudulent items related to your company that are the result of identity theft. [Consumers should redact information that is unrelated to the dispute with this company.] Also enclosed is a copy of the FTC Notice to Furnishers of Information, which details your responsibilities as an information furnisher to credit reporting agencies (CRAs). As a furnisher, upon receipt of a consumer's written request that encloses an Identity Theft Report, you are required to cease furnishing the information resulting from identity theft to any CRA.

The Notice also specifies your responsibilities when you receive notice from a CRA, under section 605B of the Fair Credit Reporting Act, that information you provided to the CRA may be the result of identity theft. Those responsibilities include ceasing to provide the inaccurate information to any CRAs and ensuring that you do not attempt to sell or transfer the fraudulent debts to another party for collection.

Please investigate this matter, close the account and absolve me of all charges, take the steps required under the Fair Credit Reporting Act, and send me a letter explaining your findings and actions.

Sincerely,
[Your Name]

Enclosures: [List what you are enclosing]

- Identity Theft Report

- Credit report of [Consumer's Name] identifying information not to be reported
- FTC Notice to Furnishers of Information

Attorney §§ 605B and 623(a)(6)(B) Dispute Letter for Furnisher
Re: New or Existing Accounts

[Date]

[Attorney's Name and Company Heading]

[Name of Company]
[Fraud Department (companies may specify an address for fraud dispute letters), or Billing Inquiries Department]
[Address]
[City, State, Zip Code]

RE: [Your ID Theft Client's Name]
         [Your Client's Account Number (if known)]

Dear Sir or Madam:

I am writing on behalf of my client, [Client's Name], concerning [his/her] notification to your company that [he/she] was the victim of identity theft. [His/her] letter, dated on [date] requested that you close the account, absolve [Client's Name] of the unauthorized debt, notify the consumer reporting agencies that the information you furnished is inaccurate and is the result of identity theft, and cease furnishing the fraudulent information to any credit reporting agency. [Client's Name] accompanied [his/her] letter with an Identity Theft Report and proof of [his/her] identity. My client requested a letter from you stating that you have taken all of the above-requested actions. [If possible: Enclosed for your reference is a copy of that letter and attachments thereto].

> [Insert facts]:
>
> Example: The credit card used to charge these disputed items was used by someone else, without my client's knowledge or permission.
>
> Example: The credit card used to purchase these items was opened without my client's authorization, by someone else using my client's personal information without [his/her] knowledge or permission.

My client reports that [summarize the nature of the problem relating to the client's request].

> Scenario 1: [Company's Name] refused to close the account and absolve the client of the debt.
>
> -or-
>
> Scenario 2: [Company's Name] continues to report the fraudulent debt to the consumer reporting companies.

-or-

Scenario 3: [Company's Name] has sold the debt to another party who is attempting to collect the debts.

-or-

Scenario 4: [Company's name] failed to provide my client with a letter stating that it has: a) closed the account and will not sell or transfer the debt to another party, b) absolved [Client's Name] from the unauthorized debt, c) notified the credit reporting agencies that the information it furnished was inaccurate and was the result of identity theft, and d) ceased furnishing the fraudulent information to any credit reporting agency.

[If the consumer provided an Identity Theft Report to the furnisher:]

As I am sure you are aware, under section 623(a)(6)(B) of the FCRA, a company that provided information to a credit reporting agency (CRA) such as [Company's Name] is required to cease furnishing such information to any CRA upon receipt of a written request of the consumer that encloses a copy of an Identity Theft Report.

[If the consumer provided the Identity Theft Report only to the CRA:]

As I am sure you are aware, once a credit reporting agency tells an information furnisher such as [Company's Name] that it has received an Identity Theft Report from the victim and has blocked fraudulent information in a victim's credit report, the information furnisher may not continue to report that information to the credit reporting agency (CRA). FCRA § 605B, 15 U.S.C. § 1681c-2. The information furnisher also may not sell or transfer that debt to anyone else who would try to collect it. FCRA § 615(f), 15 U.S.C. § 1681m(f).

Accordingly, please provide me with documentation within 14 days of the date of this letter stating that you a) do not and will not hold my client liable for this debt, b) have closed the account and will not sell or transfer the debt to any other party for collection, c) have ceased furnishing information resulting from identity theft to any credit reporting agency, and d) have notified the CRAs that the information furnished was inaccurate and was the result of identity theft.

I look forward to hearing from you and resolving this matter quickly. Please telephone or provide a written explanation within 14 days of the date of this letter. I can be reached at [insert phone number].

Sincerely,
[Attorney's Name]

Enclosures:

- Letter from [Client's Name] to [Credit Reporting Company's Name] dated [Insert date]

- Identity Theft [Report] or [Affidavit] of [Client's Name]

- **Proof of Identity of** [Client's Name]
- **FTC Notice to Furnishers of Information**

Dispute Letters Under §§ 611 and 623

Your clients and you can use the following letters to contact credit reporting agencies (CRAs) and companies that have furnished information about your client to the CRAs to request that they reinvestigate and correct all inaccurate information resulting from identity theft that appears on your client's credit reports.

- Consumer 611, 623 Dispute Letter for Credit Reporting Agencies
- Attorney 611, 623 Follow-up Letter for Credit Reporting Agencies
- Consumer 611, 623 Dispute Letters for Information Furnishers - Existing Accounts
- Consumer 611, 623 Dispute Letters for Information Furnishers - New Accounts
- Attorney 611, 623 Follow-up Letter for Information Furnishers

Consumer 611, 623 Dispute Letter for Credit Reporting Agencies

[Date]
[Your Name]
[Your Address]
[Your City, State, Zip Code]

(Write to each relevant credit reporting agency, one at a time:)

Equifax Consumer Fraud Division
P.O. Box 740256
Atlanta, GA 30374

　　　　-or-

Experian
P.O. Box 9532
Allen, TX 75013

　　　　-or-

TransUnion
Fraud Victim Assistance Department
P.O. Box 6790
Fullerton, CA 92834-6790

[RE: Your Account Number (if known)]

Dear Sir or Madam:

I am a victim of identity theft and I write to dispute certain information in my file resulting from the crime. I have circled the items I dispute on the attached copy of the report I received. The items I am disputing do not relate to any transactions that I have made or authorized. Please remove/correct this information at the earliest possible time.

{This/These] **item(s)** [identify item(s) disputed by name of the source, such as creditors or tax court, and identify type of item, such as credit account, judgment, etc.] [is/are] [inaccurate or incomplete] **because** [describe what is inaccurate or incomplete about each item, and why]. **As required by section 611 of the Fair Credit Reporting Act, 15 U.S.C. § 1681i, a copy of which is enclosed, I am requesting that the item(s) be removed** [or request another specific change] **to correct the information.**

[If applicable: Enclosed are copies of [describe any enclosed documentation, such as payment records, court documents] supporting my position.] **Please reinvestigate** [this/these matter(s)] **and** [delete or correct] **the disputed item(s) as soon as possible.**

Sincerely,
[Your name]

Enclosures: [List what you are enclosing]

- Copy of Credit Report
- Proof of Identity
- FCRA § 611, 15 U.S.C. § 1681i

Attorney 611, 623 Follow-up Letter for Credit Reporting Agencies

[Date]

[Attorney's Name and Company Heading]

(Write to each relevant credit reporting agency, one at a time:)

Equifax Consumer Fraud Division
P.O. Box 740256
Atlanta, GA 30374

     -or-

Experian
P.O. Box 9532
Allen, TX 75013

     -or-

TransUnion
Fraud Victim Assistance Department
P.O. Box 6790
Fullerton, CA 92834-6790

RE: [Your Identity Theft Client's Name]

       [Your Client's Account Number, if Applicable]

Dear Sir or Madam:

I write on behalf of my client, [Client's Name], a victim of identity theft, concerning [his/her] dispute of inaccurate information contained in the attached credit report. My client has already requested by letter dated [insert date] that you delete the disputed information from [his/her] credit report. My client reports that, notwithstanding [her/his] request, [summarize the nature of the problem with the company's response]. The inaccurate information is circled on the attached credit report [or describe inaccurate information].

Please take immediate steps to reinvestigate the accuracy of the information contained in the enclosed credit report, as required by section 611 of the Fair Credit Reporting Act, 15 U.S.C. § 1681i. In support of this request I have enclosed proof of the identity of [Client's Name]; and identification of the information which is the result of identity theft that should not be included in [Client's Name]'s credit report.

I look forward to hearing from you and resolving this matter quickly. Please telephone or provide a written explanation within 14 days of the date of this letter. I can be reached at [insert phone number].

Sincerely,
[Attorney's Name]

Enclosures:

- **Letter from** [Client's Name] **to** [Credit Reporting Agency's Name] **dated** [insert date]
- **Proof of Identity of** [Client's Name]
- **Credit Report of** [Client's Name] **identifying information not to be reported.**
- **FCRA § 611, 15 U.S.C. § 1681i**

Consumer 611, 623 Dispute Letters for Information Furnishers - Existing Accounts

[Date]

[Your Name]
[Your Address]
[Your City, State, Zip Code]

[Name of Company]
[Fraud Department (companies may specify an address to receive fraud dispute letters), or Billing Inquiries Department]
[Address]
[City, State, Zip Code]

[RE: Your Account Number (if known)]

Dear Sir or Madam:

I am writing to dispute [a] fraudulent charge(s) on my account in the amount(s) of $___, and posted on [dates]. I am a victim of identity theft, and I did not make [this/these] charge(s). I request that you remove the fraudulent charge(s) and any related finance charge and other charges from my account, send me an updated and accurate statement, and close the account (if applicable). I also request that you stop reporting this inaccurate information and report the correct information to all of the nationwide credit reporting agencies (CRAs) to which you provided it.

Enclosed is a copy of my FTC Identity Theft Affidavit supporting my position, and a copy of my credit report showing the fraudulent items related to your company that are the result of identity theft. [Consumers should redact information that is unrelated to the dispute with this company.] Also enclosed is a copy of the Notice to Furnishers issued by the Federal Trade Commission, which details your responsibilities under the Fair Credit Reporting Act as an information furnisher to CRAs.

Please investigate this matter and send me a written explanation of your findings and actions.

Sincerely,
[Your Name]

Enclosures: [List what you are enclosing]

- Identity Theft Affidavit

- Proof of identity

- FTC Notice to Furnishers of Information

- Credit report of [Consumer's Name] identifying information not to be reported or to be corrected

Consumer 611, 623 Dispute Letters for Information Furnishers - New Accounts

[Date]

[Your Name]
[Your Address]
[Your City, State, Zip Code]

[Name of Company]
[Fraud Department (companies may specify an address to receive fraud dispute letters), or Billing Inquiries Department]
[Address]
[City, State, Zip Code]

[RE: Your Account Number (if known)]

Dear Sir or Madam:

I am a victim of identity theft and I am writing to dispute certain information you have reported about me to the credit reporting agencies (CRAs). I have enclosed a copy of my FTC Identity Theft Affidavit and my credit report showing the items that I dispute. [Consumers should redact information from both reports that is unrelated to the dispute with this company.] Because the information you are reporting is the result of identity theft, and does not reflect my activities, I am requesting that you stop reporting this information to the CRAs pursuant to section 623(a)(1)(B) of the Fair Credit Reporting Act, 15 U.S.C. §1681s-2(a)(1)(B). I ask that you take these steps as soon as possible.

Enclosed are copies of [use this sentence if applicable and describe any additional enclosed documentation] supporting my position. Also enclosed is a copy of the Notice to Furnishers issued by the Federal Trade Commission, which details your responsibilities under the Fair Credit Reporting Act as an information furnisher to CRAs. Please cease reporting this information to the CRAs, investigate [this/these matter(s)], and delete the disputed item(s) as soon as possible.

Please send me a letter documenting the actions you have taken to absolve me of any responsibility for the information I am disputing, which resulted from the identity theft.

Sincerely,
[Your name]

Enclosures: [List what you are enclosing]

- FTC Identity Theft Affidavit
- Proof of identity

- Credit Report of [Consumer's Name] identifying information to be corrected
- FTC Notice to Furnishers of Information

Attorney 611, 623 Follow-up Letter for Information Furnishers

[Date]

[Attorney's Name and Company Heading]

[Name of Company]
[Fraud Department (companies may specify an address for fraud dispute letters), or Billing Inquiries Department]
[Address]
[City, State, Zip Code]

RE: [Your ID Theft Client's Name]
        [Your Client's Account Number (if known)]

Dear Sir or Madam:

I am writing on behalf of my client, [Client's Name], a victim of identity theft, concerning [his/her] dispute of inaccurate information contained in the attached credit report. Although my client, [Client's Name], has already written to you on [insert date] disputing this information, and established that the information was inaccurate and was the result of identity theft, you have failed to adequately investigate the fraudulent information. The inaccurate information is circled on the attached credit report and described in the attached Identity Theft Affidavit.

You are required under section 623(a) of the Fair Credit Reporting Act to investigate the accuracy of the information and cease from reporting any inaccurate information to credit reporting agencies (CRAs). Enclosed, as required by section 623(a), are documents establishing proof of [Client's Name]'s identity; and identifying the information which is the result of identity theft or fraud that should not be reported to the CRAs. Also enclosed is a copy of the Notice to Furnishers issued by the Federal Trade Commission, which details your responsibilities under the Fair Credit Reporting Act as an information furnisher to CRAs.

Please take immediate steps to ensure that [Company's Name] ceases from reporting information resulting from identity theft or fraud to the CRAs. [If the dispute concerns an existing account: Please ensure that the correct information is reported to all CRAs to which [Company's Name] provided the inaccurate information.] I look forward to hearing from you promptly regarding this request.

Sincerely,
[Attorney's Name]

Enclosures:

- Proof of Identity of [Client's Name]

- Credit Report of [Client's Name] identifying information not to be reported

- FTC Notice to Furnishers of Information

Disputing Fraudulent Transactions with Check Verification Companies

Your clients and you can use the following letters to contact check verification companies to dispute and request the correction of all inaccurate information resulting from identity theft that appears in your client's check verification reports.

- Consumer Dispute Letter to Check Verification Company
- Attorney Follow-up Letter to Check Verification Company

Consumer Dispute Letter to Check Verification Company

[Date]

[Your Name]
[Your Address]
[Your City, State, Zip Code]

[Name of Check Verification Company]
[Address]
[City, State, Zip Code]

[RE: Your Account Number (if known)]

Dear Sir or Madam:

I am a victim of identity theft and I am writing to dispute certain items in the enclosed copy of a check verification report, prepared by your company. I have circled the items in report that resulted from identity theft. Also enclosed is a copy of my Identity Theft Report setting forth the facts surrounding this incident of identity theft, and a copy of section 611 of the Fair Credit Reporting Act (FCRA), 15 U.S.C. § 1681i, which details your obligations as a consumer reporting agency to resolve these disputed items.

Item [identify item(s) disputed by name of source, such as creditors or tax court, and identify type of item, such as credit account, judgment, etc.] **is** [inaccurate or incomplete] **because** [describe what is inaccurate or incomplete and why]. Kindly immediately remove the **inaccurate item** [or request another specific change].

I ask that you investigate this matter and correct the inaccurate [or incomplete] information as soon as possible, as required by section 611 of the FCRA. Please send me written confirmation that the information has been [removed or corrected].

Sincerely,
[Your Name]

Enclosures: [List what you are enclosing]

- Check Verification Company Report
- Identity Theft Report
- FCRA § 611, 15 U.S.C. § 1681i

Attorney Follow-up Letter to Check Verification Company

[Date]

[Attorney's Name and Company Heading]

[Name of Check Verification Company]
[Address]
[City, State, Zip Code]

RE: [Your ID Theft Victim-Client's Name]
        [Your Client's Account Number (if known)]

Dear Sir or Madam:

I write on behalf of my client, [Client's Name], concerning [his/her] dispute of inaccurate information contained in [his/her] credit report. My client has already asked by letter dated [insert date], that you delete the disputed information from [his/her] file and that you cease from reporting information resulting from identity theft or fraud to the three national credit reporting agencies. Notwithstanding [her/his] request, my client reports that [summarize the nature of the problem with the company's response]. The inaccurate information is circled on the attached credit report and listed in the attached Identity Theft Report [or describe inaccurate information].

Section 611 of the Fair Credit Reporting Act (FCRA), 15 U.S.C. § 1681i, requires that your agency delete the disputed information from my client's credit report. In addition, pursuant to section 605B of the FCRA, kindly cease reporting to any nationwide credit reporting agency the information identified as the result of identity theft or fraud in my client's Identity Theft Report. Your company has four business days to cease from reporting the identified information to the three nationwide credit reporting agencies. FCRA § 605B(e), 15 U.S.C. § 1681c-2(e).

Enclosed for your reference are proof of [Client's Name] identity; a copy of the Identity Theft Report filed by [Client's Name] with the [Name] police department; and identification of the information which is the result of identity theft or fraud that should not be reported to the nationwide credit reporting agencies.

I look forward to hearing from you and resolving this matter quickly. Please telephone or provide a written explanation within 14 days of the date of this letter. I can be reached at [insert phone number].

Sincerely,
[Attorney=s Name]

Enclosures:

- **Proof of Identity of** [Client's Name]

- **Identity Theft Report of** [Client's Name]

- **Credit Report of** [Client's Name]
- FCRA § 605B(e), 15 U.S.C. § 1681c-2(e)
- FCRA § 611, 15 U.S.C. § 1681i.

Disputing Fraudulent ATM and Debit Card Transactions

Your clients and you can use the following letters to contact ATM or debit card issuers. The letters notify the companies that the consumer is a victim of identity theft and request the investigation of the fraudulent transaction(s) and restoration of all funds withdrawn as a result of identity theft.

- Consumer Dispute Letter
- Attorney Follow-up Letter
- Attorney Follow-up Letter After 45 Days

Consumer Dispute Letter

[Date]

[Your Name]
[Your Address]
[Your City, State, Zip Code]

[Name of Company]
[Address]
[City, State, Zip Code]

RE: Notice of stolen/lost [or unauthorized use of] ATM/Debit Card Account Number
        [Your account number (if known)]

Dear Sir or Madam:

I am the victim of identity theft. My ATM/Debit card was lost or stolen [or was used for an unauthorized transaction] on [insert date]. I did not authorize any transactions on or after this date, and I did not authorize anyone else to use my ATM/Debit card in any way.

I am notifying you, pursuant to the Electronic Fund Transfer Act, and implementing Regulation E, 15 U.S.C. § 1693 et seq., 12 C.F.R. § 205, of my lost [or stolen] ATM/Debit Card [or unauthorized transaction]. See especially 12 C.F.R. §§ 205.6, 205.11. I request that you investigate any unauthorized transactions involving this card, including but not limited to the following:

[List of unauthorized transactions].

I am attaching a copy of each of the following documents to this letter:

1. A copy of the police report about the theft of my identity [if applicable, identifying the ATM/Debit card account];

2. A copy of my FTC Identity Theft Affidavit; and,

3. The FTC Notice to Furnishers of Information

Please close the account [if applicable] and restore any funds which have been withdrawn from my account [if applicable]. Please also notify me in writing of the results of your investigation or if you have any questions regarding this notice or my requests. [As applicable] Please send me written confirmation that [any funds have been restored] and [the account has been closed].

Sincerely,
[Your Name]

Enclosures: [List what you are enclosing]

- Police Report

- FTC Identity Theft Affidavit
- FTC Notice to Furnishers of Information

Attorney Follow-up Letter

[Date]

[Attorney's Name and Company Heading]

[Name of Company]
[Address]
[City, State, Zip Code]

RE: [Client's Name] Notice of stolen/lost [or unauthorized use of] ATM/Debit card
[Your Client's Account Number (if known)]

Dear Sir or Madam:

I represent [Client's Name], who is the victim of identity theft. On [insert date] [Client's Name] notified you in writing that [his/her] ATM/Debit card was lost or stolen [or was used for an unauthorized transaction] on [provide dates of unauthorized use]. As indicated in [Client's Name]'s letter, [he/she] did not authorize any transactions on or after this date, and did not authorize anyone else to use [his/her] ATM/Debit card in any way. Notwithstanding the letter from my client, you have failed to [close the account/credit unauthorized charges or withdrawals].

Pursuant to the Electronic Funds Transfer Act, and implementing Regulation E, 15 U.S.C. § 1693 et seq., 12 C.F.R. § 205, I am writing to ask you to provide me in writing documentation of the status of your investigation. See especially 12 C.F.R. §§ 205.6, 205.11. I am also writing to reassert my client's request that you close [Client's Name]'s account and restore any funds that were improperly withdrawn from [his or her] account.

I have attached the following documents to this letter:

1.   A copy of [Client's Name]'s letter notifying you of [his/her] lost [or stolen ATM/Debit card [or unauthorized transaction, if applicable];

2.   The police report about the theft of [Client's Name]'s identity [if applicable] identifying the ATM/Debit card account, and

3.   A copy of [Client's Name]'s FTC Identity Theft Affidavit.

[Client's Name]'s identifying information is:

1.   Client's Name:

2.   Address:

3.   Phone number:

Sincerely,
[Attorney's Name]

Enclosures:

- [Client's Name] notification letter
- Police Report of [Client's Name]
- FTC Identity Theft Affidavit of [Client's Name]

Attorney Follow-up Letter After 45 Days

[Date]

[Attorney's Name and Company Heading]

[Name of Company]
[Address]
[City, State, Zip Code]

RE: [Client's Name] Notice of stolen/lost [or unauthorized use of] ATM/Debit card
[Your Client's Account Number (if known)]

Dear Sir or Madam:

I represent [Client's Name], who is the victim of identity theft. On [insert date] [Client's Name] notified you in writing that [his/her] ATM/Debit card was lost or stolen [or was used for an unauthorized transaction] on [insert date]. [Client's Name] requested that your institution investigate the unauthorized use of [his/her] ATM/Debit card, including the error in [his/her] account and restore funds that were withdrawn from [his/her] account as a result of the unauthorized use.

Notwithstanding his/her request, you failed to restore the funds that were withdrawn without authorization by my client. By this letter, I am requesting that you [credit the consumer's account or take other steps to remedy the dispute], as required by the Electronic Fund Transfer Act (EFTA), and implementing Regulation E, 15 U.S.C. § 1693 et seq.,12 C.F.R. § 205. See generally 12 C.F.R. §§ 205.6, 205.11.

As you are aware, if [Financial Institution=s Name] is unable to complete its investigation of the alleged error within ten business days after receiving notice of error, and its investigation takes up to **45** days to complete in most circumstances, [Financial Institution's Name] must provisionally credit [Client's Name]'s account within ten business days after receipt of the notice of error. 12 C.F.R. § 205.11(c)(1). Any errors must be corrected within one day after the determination that an error has occurred. 12 C.F.R. § 205.11(c)(1)-(2).

[Client's Name] **properly notified you** (Choose applicable paragraph) **[within two business days that [his/her] ATM/Debit card was lost or stolen after [he/she] realized [his/her] card was missing];**

> -or-

[within 60 days after [his/her] statement that reflected unauthorized use was mailed to [him/her] that [his/her] ATM/Debit card was lost or stolen (or that there was an incident of unauthorized use)].

Notwithstanding this timely notice, you failed to credit [his/her] **account for the funds at issue.**

Based on the notice provided by [Client's Name], and [his/her] request that you investigate the error in [his/her] account, I am reasserting [his/her] request that you credit [his/her] account with the funds that were improperly withdrawn from [his/her] account. If you refuse to credit [Client's Name]'s account because you have determined there was no error, please explain in writing your institution's findings. Please also provide the copies of documents your institution relied upon in making its determination there was no error. This request is made pursuant to 12 C.F.R. § 205.11(d)(1).

Please also state whether you have [if applicable] closed [Client's Name]'s account. I have attached the following documents to this letter:

1. A copy of [Client's Name]'s letter notifying you of [his/her] lost or stolen ATM/Debit card [or unauthorized transaction, if applicable];
2. The police report about the theft of [Client's Name]'s identity [if applicable] identifying the ATM/Debit card account; and
3. A copy of [Client's Name]'s FTC Identity Theft Affidavit.

Client's identifying information:

1. Client's Name,

2. Account number,

3. Address, and

4. Phone number.

Sincerely,
[Attorney's Name]

Enclosures:

- [Client's Name] notification letter

- Police Report of [Client's Name]

- Identity Theft Affidavit of [Client's Name]

Credit Card Issuer Obligations under the FCBA

Your clients and you can use the following letters to contact credit card issuers. The letters notify the companies that the consumer is a victim of identity theft and request that the fraudulent charges be removed and an accurate billing statement be provided.

- Consumer Letter to Credit Card Companies re: FCBA

- Attorney Follow-up Credit Card Companies re: FCBA

Consumer Letter to Credit Card Companies re: FCBA

[Date]

[Your Name]
[Your Address]
[Your City, State, Zip Code]

[Name of Creditor]
[Fraud Department (companies may specify an address to receive fraud dispute letters), or Billing Inquiries Department]
[Address]
[City, State, Zip Code]

[Re: Your Account Number (if known)]

Dear Sir or Madam:

I am writing to dispute a fraudulent charge on my account in the amount of $_____. I am a victim of identity theft, and I did not make or authorize this charge. I am requesting that the charge be removed, that any finance and other charges related to the fraudulent amount be credited, as well, and that I receive an accurate statement. This request is made pursuant to the Fair Credit Billing Act's amendments to the Truth in Lending Act, 15 U.S.C. §§ 1666-1666b, 12 C.F.R. § 226.13. See also 12 C.F.R. § 226.12(b).

Enclosed are copies of [use this sentence to describe any enclosed information, such as sales slips, payment records] supporting my position. Please investigate this matter and correct the billing error as soon as possible.

Sincerely,

[Your name]

Enclosures:

- [List what you are enclosing.]

Attorney Follow-up Credit Card Companies re: FCBA

[Date]

[Attorney's Name and Company Heading]

[Name of Credit Card Company]
[Address]
[City, State, Zip Code]

RE: [Your Client's Name]
        [Your Client's Account Number (if known)]

Dear Sir or Madam:

I am writing on behalf of my client, [Client's Name], a victim of identity theft, to follow-up on [his/her] letter to you sent on [insert date] regarding a billing error. [Client's Name] wrote to dispute a billing error in the amount of $_____ on [his/her] account. The amount is inaccurate because [describe the problem]. I am reasserting [Client's Name]'s request you correct this error, credit any finance and other charges related to the disputed amount be credited, and provide an accurate statement of the account in question. This request is made pursuant to the Fair Credit Billing Act's amendments to the Truth in Lending Act, 15 U.S.C. §§ 1666-1666b, 12 C.F.R. § 226.13. See also 12 C.F.R. § 226.12(b).

Enclosed are copies of [use this sentence to describe any enclosed information, such as letter from client, payment records, police reports, etc.] supporting my client's position. Please correct the billing error as soon as possible, and send me a letter documenting your findings and actions.

Sincerely,
[Attorney's Name]

Enclosures: [List what you are enclosing]

- **Letter from** [Client's Name] **to** [Company's Name] **dated** [insert date]
- **Police Report of** [Client's Name]

Disputing Fraudulent Charges and New Accounts with Other Creditors

Your clients and you can use the following letters to contact creditors who are not credit card issuers and do not furnish information to the credit reporting agencies, and thus are not covered by the Fair Credit Billing Act or the Fair Credit Reporting Act. (Telephone, cable, and other service providers might fit into this category.) The letters notify the companies that the consumer is a victim of identity theft and request that the fraudulent charges be removed from the victim's account, an accurate billing statement be provided, and that the account be closed, as applicable.

- Consumer Dispute Letters - Existing Accounts

- Consumer Dispute Letters - New Accounts

- Attorney Follow-up Letter

Consumer Dispute Letters - Existing Accounts

[Date]

[Your Name]
[Your Address]
[Your City, State, Zip Code]

[Name of Company]
[Fraud Department (companies may specify an address to receive fraud dispute letters, or Billing Inquiries Department]
[Address]
[City, State, Zip Code]

[Re: Your Account Number (if known)]

Dear Sir or Madam:

I am writing to dispute [a] fraudulent charge(s) on my account in the amount of $___, and posted on [provide dates]. I am a victim of identity theft, and I did not make [this/these] charge(s). Because these are not my charges, I request that you remove the fraudulent charge(s) and any related finance charge and other charges from my account, send me an updated and accurate statement, and close the account. I also request that you not sell or transfer the debt to any third party for collection.

Enclosed is proof of my identity and my Identity Theft Affidavit, setting out as much as I know of the circumstances under which this fraudulent charge was made, [and other material] establishing the fraud. [Consumers should redact information that is unrelated to the dispute with this company.]

Please investigate this matter, correct the fraudulent charge(s), and send me a written explanation of your findings and actions.

Sincerely,
[Your Name]

Enclosures: [List what you are enclosing]

- Proof of Identity

- Identity Theft Affidavit

- Supporting Documentation [specify]

Consumer Dispute Letters - New Accounts

[Date]

[Your Name]
[Your Address]
[Your City, State, Zip Code]

[Name of Company]
[Fraud Department (companies may specify an address to receive fraud dispute letters), or Billing Inquiries Department]
[Address]
[City, State, Zip Code]

[Re: Your Account Number (if known)]

Dear Sir or Madam:

I am a victim of identity theft. I recently learned that my personal information was used to open an account at your company. I did not open or authorize this account, and request that you close the account immediately. I also request that you absolve me of all charges on the account, and further that you not sell or transfer the account to any third party for collection.

Enclosed is a copy of my proof of identity and my Identity Theft Affidavit establishing the fraud and supporting my position.

Please investigate this matter, close the account and absolve me of all charges, and send me a letter explaining your findings and actions.

Sincerely,
[Your Name]

Enclosures: [List what you are enclosing]

- Proof of identity
- Identity Theft Affidavit

Attorney Follow-up Letter

[Date]

[Attorney's Name and Company Heading]
[Name of Company]
[Address]
[City, State, Zip Code]

RE: [Your ID Theft Client's Name]
        [Your Client's Account Number (if known)]

Dear Sir or Madam:

I am writing on behalf of my client, [Client's Name], concerning [his/her] notification to your company that [he/she] was the victim of identity theft. [His/her] letter, dated [insert date] requested that you close the account, absolve [Client's Name] of the unauthorized debt, and not sell or transfer the debt to any other party for collection. [Client's Name] accompanied [his/her] letter with an Identity Theft Affidavit and proof of [his/her] identity. My client requested a letter from you stating that you have taken all of the above-requested actions. [If possible: Enclosed for your reference is a copy of my client's letter and attachments thereto.] Notwithstanding [her/his] request, you have not [closed the account, absolved the debt, etc.] By this letter, I am asking you to resolve this situation according to my client's request.

Explanation of facts:

Example: The account was used to by someone else, without my client's knowledge or permission.

Example: The account was opened without my client's authorization, by someone else using my client's personal information without their knowledge or permission.

My client reports that [summarize the nature of the problem relating to the client's request].

Scenario 1: [Company's Name] refused to close the account and absolve the client of the debt.

or

Scenario 2: [Company's Name] has sold the debt to another party who is attempting to collect the debts.

-or-

Scenario 3: [Company's name] failed to provide my client with a letter stating that your company has closed the account, absolved [Client's Name] of the unauthorized debt, and will not sell or transfer the debt to another party.

Please provide me with documentation stating that you do not and will not hold my client liable for this debt, have closed the account, and will not sell or transfer the debt to any other party for collection.

I look forward to hearing from you and resolving this matter quickly. Please telephone or provide a written explanation including the documentation requested above within 14 days of the date of this letter. I can be reached at [insert phone number].

Sincerely,
[Attorney's Name]

Enclosures: [List what you are enclosing]

- **Letter from** [Client's Name] **to** [Creditor] **dated** [Insert date]
- **Identity Theft Affidavit of** [Client's Name]
- **Proof of Identity of** [Client's Name]

Disputing Debts Resulting From Identity Theft with Debt Collectors

Your clients and you can use the following letters to contact debt collectors. The letters notify the debt collectors that the consumer is a victim of identity theft and request that the debt collector take the actions required under the Fair Debt Collections Practices Act and the Fair Credit Reporting Act.

- Consumer Letter to Debt Collector
- Attorney Letter to Debt Collector

Consumer Letter to Debt Collector

[Date]

[Your Name]
[Your Address]
[Your City, State, Zip Code]

[Name of Credit Collection Agency]
[Address]
[City, State, Zip Code]

[Re: Your Account Number (if known)]

Dear Sir or Madam:

I am the victim of identity theft. I recently learned that someone used my personal information to open an account and make purchases with [Creditor's Name]. This debt is not mine. In accordance with the Fair Debt Collection Practices Act, I request that you stop collection proceedings against me and cease communications with me about this debt, except to comply with section 615(g)(2) of the Fair Credit Reporting Act (FCRA), as described below. I further request, pursuant to section 615(g)(1) of the FCRA, that you notify [Creditor's Name] that the debt is the result of identity theft.

[Explanation].

> Example: The credit card used to charge these items was opened without my authorization by someone using my sensitive personally identifying information.

Enclosed is a copy of the Notice to Furnishers of Information issued by the Federal Trade Commission, which details your responsibilities under the FCRA as an information furnisher to credit reporting agencies. The Notice also specifies your responsibilities when a credit reporting agency notifies you under section 605B of the FCRA that information you provided to it may be the result of identity theft.

Section 615(g)(2) of the FCRA requires debt collectors to provide identity theft victims with documentation about an account if the victim asks for it. Please provide me with the following documents related to this account:

1. Application records or screen prints of Internet/phone applications
2. Statements or invoices
3. Payment/charge slips
4. Investigator's summary
5. Delivery addresses
6. All records of phone numbers used to activate or access the account
7. Signatures on applications and accounts
8. Any other documents or records associated with the account

Please send me a letter detailing the actions you have taken to:

1. notify the original creditor that the debt is the result of identity theft;
2. stop collection proceedings against me;
3. cease reporting this information to the credit reporting agencies;
4. provide me with the information I am requesting; and
5. take all actions required of you as a furnisher of information to credit reporting agencies.

Thank you for your cooperation.

Sincerely,
[Your Name]

Enclosures: [List what you are enclosing]

- Proof of Identity
- FCRA § 615(g)(2)
- FTC Notice to Furnishers of Information

Attorney Letter to Debt Collector

[Date]

[Attorney's Name and Company Heading]

[Name of Debt Collector]
[Address]
[City, State, Zip Code]

RE: [Your Client's Name]
        [The Account Number Opened or Misused by the Identity Thief (if known)]

Dear Sir or Madam:

I am writing on behalf of my client, [Client's Name], a victim of identity theft, concerning the referenced debt. You have attempted to collect on this debt, but, as set out further below, this is not my client's debt.

This letter follows an earlier letter to you from my client, dated [insert date], requesting that you [add detail] but you nonetheless [add detail]. By this letter I am requesting that you cease communications with [him/her] about the debt, except to comply with section 615(g)(2) of the Fair Credit Reporting Act (FCRA), and stop all collection proceedings against [him/her].

As outlined below, this is not my client's debt.

[Insert explanation of why it is not your client's debt (example below).]

> Example: The credit card used to charge these items was opened without my client's authorization by someone using [his/her] name and Social Security number, and other personal information.

In accordance with section 805(c) of the Fair Debt Collection Practices Act (FDCPA), my client has requested in writing that you cease communications with [him/her] about the debt you are attempting to collect and stop all collection proceedings. Pursuant to section 615(g) of the

FCRA, my client also requested that you notify the creditor that this account is the result of identity theft, and that you provide my client with all documentation relating to this account.

My client provided you a copy of the Notice to Furnishers of Information issued by the Federal Trade Commission. The Notice specifies that when a credit reporting agency notifies you, under section 605B of the FCRA, that information you provided to it may be the result of identity theft, you may not sell or transfer the debt or place it for collection. You also must stop reporting that information to any credit reporting agency.

Problem 1: Debt Collector Continues To Communicate With Client

Although [Client's Name] notified you that [he/she] is the victim of identity theft, and requested in writing that you cease communications about the fraudulent debt, your company continues to communicate with my client about the debt. Section 805(c) of the FDCPA prohibits a debt collector from contacting a consumer about a debt (with certain exceptions that do not apply in this case) upon receipt of the consumer's written request. I request that you immediately halt all communications with my client to collect on this fraudulent debt.

Problem 2: Debt Collector Continues Collection Attempts Other Than Communications with Client (e.g., Filing Suit or Reporting Account to Credit Reporting Agency)

Although my client notified you in writing, within the 30-day dispute period, that [he/she] disputes the debt because [he/she] is a victim of identity theft, you have continued collection efforts by [reporting the account to a credit reporting agency] [filing suit to collect the alleged debt]. Section 809(b) of the FDCPA requires a debt collector to suspend collection efforts upon timely notification of a dispute by the consumer. I request that immediate steps be taken to halt all attempts to collect on this fraudulent debt, until you have provided [Client's Name] with proper proof of the debt.

Problem 3: Debt Collector Has Not Notified Creditor

Although my client notified you that [he/she] is the victim of identity theft, the creditor associated with this debt continues to attempt to collect the fraudulent debt. Section 615(g)(1) of the FCRA requires debt collectors who have received a notice of identity theft to notify the creditor that the debt may be fraudulent. Accordingly, I request that you take immediate steps to alert the creditor that this debt is the result of identity theft.

Problem 4: Debt Collector Has Not Provided Requested Documentation

Although my client asked you to provide documentation about the account pursuant to section 615(g)(2) of the FCRA, you have not done so. Please provide me and my client with the following documents pertaining to the fraudulent debt:

1. Application records or screen prints of Internet or phone applications
2. Statements or invoices
3. Payment/charge slips
4. Investigator's summary
5. Delivery addresses
6. All records of phone numbers used to activate or access the account
7. Signatures on applications and accounts
8. Any other documents or records associated with the account

I look forward to hearing from you and resolving this matter quickly. Please call or provide a written explanation within 14 days of the date of this letter. I can be reached at [insert phone number].

Sincerely,
[Attorney's Name]

Enclosures: [List what you are enclosing]

- **Letter from** [Client's name] **to** [Debt Collector's name] **dated** [insert date]
- **Enclosures sent by the client** [specify]
- FCRA § 615(g), FDCPA §§ 805(c), 809(b)
- FTC's Notice to Furnishers of Information

Obtaining Business Records Relating to Identity Theft

You, your client, and law enforcement officers designated by the victims can use these letters to contact companies that have transacted business with someone who has fraudulently used the victim's personally identifying information. The letters notify the company that the consumer is a victim of identity theft and request that it provide copies of application and business transaction records related to the identity theft to the designated parties.

- Consumer Request Letter
- Law Enforcement Request Letter
- Attorney Follow-up Letter

Consumer Request Letter

[Date]

[Your Name]
[Your Address]
[Your City, State, Zip Code]

[Name of Company]
[Address specified by the company for 609(e) requests, or, if none is specified, the address for the Fraud Department or Billing Inquiries Department]
[City, State, Zip Code]

RE: Request for Records Pursuant to Section 609(e) of the Fair Credit Reporting Act
        [Description of fraudulent transaction/account]
        [Dates of fraudulent transaction or Account Number (if known)]

Dear Sir or Madam:

I am a victim of identity theft. The thief [made a fraudulent transaction/opened a fraudulent account] in my name with your company. In accordance with section 609(e) of the Fair Credit Reporting Act, 15 U.S.C. § 1681g(e), I am requesting that you provide me copies of business records relating to the fraudulent [transaction/account] identified above. The law directs that you provide these documents at no charge, and without requiring a subpoena, within thirty (30) days of your receipt of this request. I am enclosing a copy of the relevant federal law and the Federal Trade Commission's business education publication on this topic.

Enclosed with this request is the following documentation, as applicable:

1. Proof of my identity: A copy of my driver's license, other government-issued identification card, or other proof of my identity; and

2. Proof of my claim of identity theft:

    - A copy of the police report about my identity theft; and

    - A completed and signed FTC Identity Theft Affidavit or alternative affidavit of fact.

Please provide all records relating to the fraudulent [transaction/account], including:

- Application records or screen prints of internet/phone applications

- Statements/invoices

- Payment/charge slips

- Investigator's summary

- Delivery addresses

- All records of phone numbers used to activate or access the account

- Any other documents associated with the account

Please send these records to me at the above address.

[If applicable: In addition, I authorize the law enforcement officer who is investigating my case to submit this request on my behalf and/or receive copies of these records from you. The law enforcement officer's name, address and telephone number is: [insert officer name, address and telephone]. Please also send copies of all records to this officer.

If you have any questions concerning this request, please contact me at the above address or at [your telephone number].

Sincerely,

[Your Name]

Enclosures: [List only those items that you are enclosing]

- A copy of the law: FCRA § 609(e) (15 U.S.C. § 1681g(e))

- A copy of "*Businesses Must Provide Victims and Law Enforcement with Transaction Records Relating to Identity Theft*"

- A copy of my driver's license, other government-issued identification card, or other proof of identity

- A copy of the police report

- My FTC Identity Theft Affidavit or alternative affidavit of fact

Law Enforcement Request Letter

To:

Regarding: Account Number:
                Name on Account:

Description of fraudulent [transaction/account]:

From: [Law Enforcement Officer's Name]
       [Law Enforcement Agency's Name]
       [Agency/Department Address]
       [Telephone Number]

I am contacting you on behalf of an identity theft victim, [Victim's Name], whose case I am investigating. [Victim's Name]'s personal information was used by someone else to make a fraudulent transaction or open a fraudulent account with your company. In accordance with section 609(e) of the Fair Credit Reporting Act, I am requesting that you provide me copies of application and business records relating to the fraudulent [transaction/account] identified above. The victim's letter authorizing me to receive copies of such documents is enclosed. Federal law provides that, upon request of the victim, you make these documents available to me, as a law enforcement officer, free and without the need to issue a subpoena.

Please provide all information relating to the fraudulent account or transaction, including:

- Application records or screen prints of Internet/phone applications
- Statements/invoices
- Payment/charge slips
- Investigator's summary
- Delivery addresses
- All records of phone numbers used to activate the account or used to access the account
- Any other documents associated with the account.

Please send the information to me at the above address. You can contact me at [telephone number] if you need further information.

Enclosure:

- Request Letter of [Victim's name] Authorizing Law Enforcement Officer to Receive Fraudulent Transaction/Account Information, dated [insert date], with Victim's Enclosures

Attorney Follow-up Letter

[Date]

[Attorney's Name and Company Heading]

[Name of Company]
[Address]
[City, State, Zip Code]

RE: [Your Client's Name]
       [The Account Number Affected or Opened in Your Client's Name (if known)]

Dear Sir or Madam:

I write on behalf of my client, [Client's Name], concerning [his/her] request that you provide [him/her] the application and transaction documents related to [his/her] identity theft as required by section 609(e) of the Fair Credit Reporting Act (FCRA). (If appropriate, insert: [Client's Name] also requested that you provide copies for the designated law enforcement officer who is investigating [his/her] case.)

My client made this request in a letter to you dated [insert date], accompanied by a police report, my client's FTC Identity Theft Affidavit, and proof of [his/her] identity. [If possible: Enclosed for your reference is a copy of that letter and attachments thereto.] My client reports that you have refused to provide the requested documents without first receiving a subpoena.

Under section 609(e) of the FCRA, a victim of identity theft is entitled to the above-referenced documents without a subpoena. This law requires that a company provide copies of the application and business transaction records in its control to the victim and their law enforcement designee, within 30 days of receipt of a request from the victim when it has provided credit, products, goods, or services to, accepted payment from, or otherwise entered into a commercial transaction with, a person who has allegedly made unauthorized use of the means of identification of the victim. FCRA § 609(e)(1), 15 U.S.C. § 1681g(e)(1).

It appears that [Company's Name]'s failure to provide the requested documentation does not comply with the requirements of the FCRA. Therefore, please provide me with copies of the application for the account and the transaction records concerning this fraudulent debt. Relevant documents should include, but are not limited to, the following types of records:

- Application records or screen prints of Internet/phone applications
- Billing statements
- Payment/charge slips
- Investigator's summary
- Delivery addresses
- All records of phone numbers used to activate or access the account

- Signatures on applications and accounts

- Any other documents or records associated with the account

[If appropriate: [Client's Name] also authorizes the provision of these documents free of charge to the law enforcement officer listed below.

[Police or Sheriff's Department]
[Law Enforcement Officer's Name]
[Address]
[City, State, Zip Code]
[Identity Theft Report No:_____]]

I would be happy to discuss this matter in a phone call. If you believe you are not required to provide any part of the documentation requested in this letter, please provide me with a written explanation of your position within 14 days of the date of this letter. I look forward to hearing from you and resolving this matter quickly.

Sincerely,
[Attorney's Name]

Enclosures: [List what you are enclosing]

- **Proof of identity of** [Client's Name]

- **Letter from** [Client's Name] **to** [Company's Name] **dated** [insert date]

- **Police Report of** [Client's Name]

- **Identity Theft Affidavit of** [Client's Name]

- 15 U.S.C. § 1681g(e)

Appendix D:
Core Consumer Educational Materials

This section contains important information for identity theft victims, primarily from the FTC. There are many cross references to these materials throughout the Guide.

You may want to keep a supply of these resources on hand to send to victims after their initial screening phone call, or to give them during the intake interview. You can place bulk order requests for most of these resources from the FTC's. They are free.

Recommended Identity Theft Materials

Key Information for all Victims

- Statement of Rights for Identity Theft Victims
- Immediate Steps to Repair Identity Theft
- Identity Theft: What to Know, What to Do (PDF brochure)
- Taking Charge: What To Do If Your Identity Is Stolen (PDF booklet)
- Action Plan for Identity Theft Victims (from VICARS)
- Understanding & Creating an ID Theft Report

Specific Types of Identity Theft

- Safeguarding Your Child's Future
- Tax Related Identity Theft
- Medical Identity Theft

More

- Identity Theft Protection Services
- Free Credit Reports
- How to Read a Credit Report (from cccsoc.org)
- Businesses Must Provide Victims and Law Enforcement with Transaction Records

Appendix E:
Federal Statutes and Regulations

- Identity Theft and Assumption Deterrence Act of 1998, 18 U.S.C. § 1028(a)7; and Pub. Law 105-318, 112 Stat. 3068

- Identity Theft Enforcement and Restitution Act of 2008, Pub. Law 110-326, Title II, 122 Stat. 3560

The Fair Credit Reporting Act (FCRA)

- Fair Credit Reporting Act, 15 U.S.C. § 1681

- FTC Notice to Furnishers under FCRA, 74 Fed. Reg. 31,484 (July 1, 2009)

- FCRA § 605B, 15 U.S.C. § 1681c-2, Blocking Information on Credit Reports

- FCRA § 609(e), 15 U.S.C. § 1681g, Business Documents Available to Victims

- FCRA § 611, 15 U.S.C. § 1681i, Disputing Information on Credit Reports

- FCRA § 615(f), 15 U.S.C. § 1681m(f), Prohibition on Sale of Debt Caused by Identity Theft

- FCRA § 615(g), 15 U.S.C. § 1681m(g), Debt Collector Communications Concerning Identity Theft

- FCRA § 623(a)(6) , 15 U.S.C. § 1681s-2, Duties of Information Furnishers upon Notice of Identity Theft

Other Statues & Regulations

- 16 C.F.R. Part 602 - Fair and Accurate Credit Transactions Act of 2003

- 16 C.F.R. Part 603 - Definitions - Identity Theft; Identity Theft Report

- Final Rule on Related Identity Theft Definitions, 69 Fed. Reg. 63,922 (November 3, 2004)

- 12 C.F.R. 1022.130-139 (formerly 69 Fed. Reg. 35,468) Fair Credit Reporting (Regulation V), Subpart N, Duties of Consumer Reporting Agencies regarding Disclosure to Consumers

- 16 C.F.R. Part 614 - Appropriate Proof of Identity

- Fair Credit Billing Act, 15 U.S.C. § 1601

- Fair Debt Collection Practices Act, § 805(c) & 809(b), 15 U.S.C. § 1692(c), (g)

- Electronic Funds Transfer Act, 12 C.F.R. § 205

- <u>34 C.F.R. § 682.402(e)(14) – Regulations of the Offices of the Department of Education</u>
- <u>34 C.F.R. § 685.215(c)(4) – Regulations of the Offices of the Department of Education</u>

www.ingramcontent.com/pod-product-compliance
Lightning Source LLC
Chambersburg PA
CBHW080259180526
45167CB00006B/2586